Son of God

A Bible Study for Women on the Gospel of Mark (Volume 1)

Mark 1:1 – 9:13

Keri Folmar

CruciformPress

CruciformPress.com | info@CruciformPress.com

Praise for Keri Folmar's Inductive Bible Studies for Women

"With simple clarity, Keri Folmar guides us in learning to study the Bible…Keri encourages us to read God's Word carefully, to understand clearly, and to apply prayerfully…she encourages her readers first and foremost to listen well to God's inspired Word."

Kathleen Nielson is author of the *Living Word Bible Studies*; Director of Women's Initiatives, The Gospel Coalition; and wife of Niel, who served as President of Covenant College, 2002 to 2012.

"Keri's Bible study will not only bring the truths of [Scripture] to bear upon your life, but will also train you up for better, more effective study of any book of the Bible with her consistent use of the three questions needed in all good Bible study: Observation, Interpretation, and Application."

Connie Dever is author of *The Praise Factory* children's ministry curriculum and wife of Mark, senior pastor of Capitol Hill Baptist Church and President of 9Marks.

"It is hard to imagine a better inductive Bible study tool than this one. So many study tools wander from the biblical text, but Keri Folmar's study concentrates on what [the biblical author] says... unfolding its message with accuracy and clarity."

Diane Schreiner, the wife of SBTS professor, author, and pastor Tom Schreiner and mother of four grown children, has led women's Bible studies for more than 20 years.

"No clever stories, ancillary anecdotes, or emotional manipulation here. Keri takes us deeper into the text, deeper into the heart of [the biblical author], deeper into the mind of Christ, and deeper into our own hearts… a great study to do on your own or with others."

Kristie Anyabwile is a North Carolina native and graduate of NC State University with a degree in history. Her husband, Thabiti, serves as a pastor in Washington, DC, and as a Council Member for The Gospel Coalition.

"Keri is convinced that God is God-centered and that for the sake of our joy, we should be, too…She skillfully created these rich resources—and not only that, she has put the tools in your hands so you can study God's word for yourself…I highly recommend that you embark on these studies with some other ladies. Then you can all watch in amazement at how God gives you contentment in him."

Gloria Furman is a pastor's wife in the Middle East, and author of *Glimpses of Grace*, *Treasuring Christ When Your Hands Are Full*, and *The Pastor's Wife.*

Table of Contents

Don't miss these fully inductive Bible studies for women from Keri Folmar!

10 weeks

Joy! (Philippians)

10 weeks

Faith (James)

10 weeks

Grace (Ephesians)

11 weeks

11 weeks

Son of God (Gospel of Mark, 2 volumes)

9 weeks

Zeal (Titus)

Son of God - A Bible Study for Women on the Gospel of Mark (Volume 1)

Print / PDF ISBN: 978-1-941114-79-7

Published by Cruciform Press, Minneapolis, Minnesota. Italics or bold text within Scripture quotations indicates emphasis added.

Introduction: Why Study the Bible?

As we begin this study of the Gospel of Mark, we should think through why we are studying the Bible. Why not read some other book? Or why not just get together with some other women and chat?

Well, have you heard the story about the kindergarten teacher who had her class paint pictures of anything they chose? After observing a little girl who was working very intently on her painting, the teacher asked, "What are you painting?" The girl answered, "It's a picture of God." Amused, the teacher informed her, "No one knows what God looks like." Without looking up from her painting, the little girl responded, "They will in a minute!"

This might be a cute example of a precocious child, but many people paint pictures of God in their own minds. They "know" that God is a certain way, because they want him to be that way.

However, the one true God is transcendent. He is beyond our capacity to know. First Timothy 6:16 describes God, "[W]ho alone has immortality, who dwells in unapproachable light, whom no one has ever seen or can see." God existed before time. He is the Creator, and we are his creatures. Sinful man cannot approach the holy God.

How can we know this God if we cannot approach him? He has to approach us. The only way to truly know God is for him to reveal himself to us. He reveals his existence and power in creation. (See Psalm 19 and Romans 1:18–21.) However, if we want to truly know God in a personal way, it must be through his Word.

And God **wants** us, his creatures, to know him. Jeremiah 10:23–24 says:

> Thus says the Lord: "Let not the wise man boast in his wisdom, let not the mighty man boast in his might, let not the rich man boast in his riches, but let him who boasts boast in this, that he understands and knows me, that I am the Lord who practices steadfast love, justice, and righteousness in the earth."

Do you boast in understanding and knowing the Lord? Do you want to know this God who practices love, justice, and righteousness in the earth? He wants you to understand and know him. He is ready to speak to you every morning when you wake up… throughout the day… and before you go to bed. You have only to open his Word.

A well-known catechism says, "The chief end of man is to glorify God and enjoy him forever." That is what we were created for—to truly know and enjoy the God of the universe. Jeremiah the prophet cried out: "Your words were found, and I ate them, and your words became to me a joy and the delight of my heart."

The great preacher, C.H. Spurgeon, said:

> Believer! There is enough in the Bible for you to live upon forever. If you should outnumber the years of Methuselah, there would be no need for a fresh revelation; if you should live until Christ should return to the earth, there would be no necessity for the addition of a single word; if you should go down as deep as Jonah, or even descend as David said he did, into the depths of hell, still there would be enough in the Bible to comfort you without a supplementary sentence. (http://spurgeon.org/sermons/0005.htm)

This is why we study the Bible: it is God's revelation of himself to us. We need to know who God truly is and guard against painting our own picture of him. God has revealed himself to us not in paintings but through his Son by the words of the Scripture. God, the creator, has spoken, and we, his creation, should listen to his words as life-sustaining truth and joyfully obey them.

This Bible study workbook is to assist you in studying the first half of the Gospel of Mark in an inductive way. Inductive study is **reading the passage in context and asking questions of the text with the purpose of deriving the meaning and significance from the text itself**. We do this automatically every day when we read the newspaper, blogs, or even recipes. When we study the Bible inductively we are after the author's original intent; i.e., what the author meant when he wrote the passage to his original audience. In this workbook, you will figure out the meaning by answering a series of questions about the text, paying close attention to the words and context of the passage. After figuring out the meaning of the text, there will be questions to help you apply it to your life.

In the Gospel of Mark, you will immerse yourself in eyewitness accounts of Jesus and read of wondrous things he said and did. As you read through Mark, may the Holy Spirit open your eyes to more deeply understand and rejoice in Jesus Christ, the Son of God.

How to Do Inductive Bible Study

Step 1 – Begin with prayer. "Open my eyes, that I may behold wondrous things out of your law" (Psalm 119:18).

Step 2 – Read the text.

Step 3 – Observation. The goal of this step is to figure out what the text is saying. These questions should be answered from the very words of the text.

Step 4 – Interpretation. The goal of this step is to figure out what the text meant to the original hearers. This most important step is often skipped, but a lack of correct interpretation leads to incorrect application. We cannot understand what God is saying to us if we don't first understand what he was saying to his original audience, and why he was saying it.

Your job in interpretation is to figure out the main point of the passage and understand the arguments that support the main point. Your interpretation should flow out of your observations, so keep asking yourself, "Can I support this interpretation based on my observations?"

Step 5 – Application. Prayerfully apply the passage to your own life. The application should flow from the main point of the text.

Keep God's Redemptive Plan in Mind

Luke 24:44–47 says,

> Then [Jesus] said to them, "These are my words that I spoke to you while I was still with you, that everything written about me in the Law of Moses

> and the Prophets and the Psalms must be fulfilled." Then he opened their minds to understand the Scriptures, and said to them, "Thus it is written, that the Christ should suffer and on the third day rise from the dead, and that repentance and forgiveness of sins should be proclaimed in his name to all nations, beginning from Jerusalem."

We study the Bible so that we can know Christ, repent, be forgiven, and proclaim him to the nations. We must keep Jesus in mind when we study Scripture. Adrienne Lawrence writes, "God has one overarching redemptive plan—to glorify himself by creating and redeeming a people for himself through Christ. Christ is at the center of God's plan. All of Scripture in some way speaks to that plan. Keep this in mind as you are doing your study of Scripture."

[Note: This "How to" has been adapted from Adrienne Lawrence's pamphlet on Inductive Bible Study.]

Notes

The first week of this inductive study will primarily be an overview of Mark. On the following days you will study smaller segments of the letter and answer observation, interpretation, and application questions. The questions were written based on language from the English Standard Version of the Bible. However, you are welcome to use any reliable translation to do the study.

To assist you in recognizing the different types of questions asked, the questions are set out with icons as indicated below.

Observation: Look closely in order to figure out what the text is saying. Get answers directly from the text, using the words of Scripture to answer the observation questions.

Interpretation: What's the "true north" for this verse? Determine the author's intended meaning by figuring out what the text meant to its original hearers.

Application: Based on the author's meaning of the text, apply the passage to your own heart and life.

Because Scripture interprets Scripture, many of the questions cite passages in addition to the one you are studying in Mark. If the question says, "Read…" you will need to read the additional verses cited to answer the question. If the question says, "See…" the verses help you answer the question but are not necessary. "See also…" signals you to read the verses if you would like to study the answer to the question further.

You only need your Bible to do this study of Mark, and, in fact, I highly recommend first answering the questions directly from your Bible before looking at any other materials. That said, it might be helpful for you to confirm your answers, especially if you are leading others in a group study. To check your answers or for further study, *The Gospel According to Mark* by James R. Edwards, Mark by R. Alan Cole, or *Mark* by J.C. Ryle, are good commentaries to use.

For more general help in knowing how to study the Bible, I highly recommend Bible Study: *Following the Ways of the Word*, by Kathleen Buswell Nielson, *Dig Deeper! Tools to Unearth the Bible's Treasure*, by Nigel Beynon and Andrew Sach, and *Knowable Word: Helping Ordinary People Learn to Study the Bible*, by Peter Krol. Bible study teachers and students who want a closer look at New Testament theology that will also encourage your heart can read Thomas Schreiner's, *Magnifying God in Christ: A Summary of New Testament Theology*. For information that explains why Christians base their life and doctrine on the Bible, see my book, *The Good Portion: The Doctrine of Scripture for Every Woman.*

Notes for Leaders

This Bible study can be done by individuals alone, but the best context for Bible study is in the local church. Studying the Bible together promotes unity and ignites spiritual growth within the church.

The study was designed for participants to complete five days of "homework," and then come together to discuss their answers in a small group. The goal of gathering in small groups is to promote discussion among women to sharpen one another by making sure all understand the meaning of the text and can apply it to their lives. As women discuss, their eyes may be opened to applications of the text they didn't see while doing the study on their own. Believers will encourage one another in their knowledge of the gospel, and unbelievers will hear the gospel clearly explained. As a result, women will learn from one another and come away from group Bible study with a deeper understanding of the text and a better knowledge of how to read the Bible on their own in their private times of study and prayer.

If you are leading a small group, you will have some extra homework to do. **First, know what Bible study is and is not.** Bible study is not primarily a place to meet felt needs, eat good food and chat, receive counseling, or have a free-for-all discussion. Some of these things do happen in a womens' Bible study, but they should not take over the focus. Bible study is digging into the Scriptures to get the true meaning of the text and applying it to lives that change as a result.

Second, make sure you know the main points of the text before leading discussion by carefully studying the passage and checking yourself using a good commentary, like one of those listed above. You may also find a Bible dictionary and concordance helpful. Second Timothy 3:16–17 says, "All Scripture is breathed out by God and profitable for teaching, for reproof, for correction, and for training in righteousness, that the man [or woman] of God may be competent, equipped for every good work." Scripture is powerful. That power comes through truth. Scripture is not like a magical incantation: We say the words and see the effect. We must know what the text of Scripture means before we apply it and see its work of transformation in our lives. Your job as a discussion leader is not to directly teach, nor to simply facilitate discussion, but rather to lead women in finding the meaning of the text and help them see how it is "profitable" and can make them "competent, equipped for every good work."

Third, pray. Pray for the women in your group during the week while you prepare. Pray as you start your small group study, asking the Holy Spirit to illuminate the Scripture to your minds and apply it to your hearts. And encourage women to pray at the end of your small group based on what they studied. Ask the Holy Sprit to use his sword, the word of God, in the lives of the women you are leading.

Fourth, draw women into discussion and keep your discussion organized. Choose what you determine are the most important questions from the study guide, focusing the bulk of your discussion on the interpretation and application questions. Ask a question, but don't answer it! Be comfortable with long pauses or rephrase questions you think the group didn't understand. Not answering the questions yourself may be a bit awkward at first, but it will promote discussion in the end because the women will know they have to do the answering. Feel free to affirm good answers or sum up after women have had time to discuss particular questions. This gives clarity to the discussion. However, don't feel the need to fill in every detail and nuance you gleaned from your personal study. Your goal is to get your group talking.

Fifth, keep your focus on the Bible. The Holy Spirit uses the Scriptures to change women's hearts. Don't be afraid of wrong answers. Gently use them to clarify and teach by directing attention back to the text of Scripture for the right answer. If someone in your group goes off on unhelpful tangents, direct her back to the question and address the tangent later, one on one, or with reading material. However, if the tangent is on a vital question that goes to the gospel, take time to talk about it. These are God-given opportunities.

Sixth, be sure you focus on the gospel. In your prep time, ask yourself what the text has to do with the gospel and look for opportunities to ask questions to bring out the gospel. Hopefully, your church members will invite unbelievers to your study who will hear the glorious good news. But, even if your group is made up of all believers, we never get beyond our need to be reminded of Christ crucified and what that means for our lives.

Lastly, enjoy studying the Scriptures with your group. Your love and passion for the word of God will be contagious, and you will have the great joy of watching your women catch it and rejoice in the word with you.

Mark

Mark, also called John Mark, was a close companion of several apostles and partnered with them in the spread of the gospel. He traveled with Paul and Barnabas at the beginning of their first missionary journey (Acts 12:25–13:13), visiting Antioch, Cyprus, Paphos and Perga. Mark then left Paul and Barnabas and returned to Jerusalem, later causing a "sharp disagreement" about whether to take Mark on a second journey with them. Barnabas ended up taking Mark with him to Cyprus, and Paul took Silas to Asia Minor. Paul was later reconciled to Mark and asked Timothy to bring Mark to visit him in jail because he considered Mark so useful to his ministry (2 Timothy 4:11; See also Colossians 4:10).

The apostle Peter goes so far as to call Mark his son (1 Peter 5:13). Peter would have known Mark from the earliest days of the church because the church met in the home of Mark's mother. In fact, this home is probably where Peter went when an angel broke him out of Herod's prison (Acts 12:12). Early church tradition is unanimous that Mark wrote his Gospel under the direction of the apostle Peter. Likely written shortly before or after Peter's death in Rome (sometime in the mid 60s AD), Mark's Gospel was probably the first Gospel written and was recognized as canonical because of its connection to Peter. Papias, an early church father who knew the apostles, said that Mark wrote down everything he heard from Peter about Jesus and included nothing false in the accounts.

Week 1

Day 1 — Overview of Mark & Mark 1:1

Begin each day this week asking God to open your eyes to Jesus and to the glory of his gospel.

The first four days of this week will be an overview of the Gospel of Mark. Each of these days we'll read through four chapters and take notes. We'll notice repeated themes and familiarize ourselves with the characters and culture of the Gospel story. Don't worry about being too detailed. We will be studying in more detail in future weeks.

Pray, then read Mark chapters 1–4.

What are some things that Jesus does in these chapters?

What statements does Jesus make about himself or what he came to do?

What surprised you or stood out to you when you read these chapters?

Who are some of the main characters involved in these Gospel accounts? (Include antagonists as well as protagonists.)

What are some things you learned about Jesus from reading these chapters?

What questions arose in your mind as you were reading?

Day 2

Pray, then read Mark chapters 5–8.

What are some things that Jesus does in these chapters?

What statements does Jesus make about himself or what he came to do?

What surprised you or stood out to you when you read these chapters?

Who are some of the main characters involved in these Gospel accounts? (Include antagonists as well as protagonists.)

What are some things your learned about Jesus from reading these chapters?

What questions arose in your mind as you were reading?

Day 3

Pray, then read Mark chapters 9–12.

What are some things that Jesus does in these chapters?

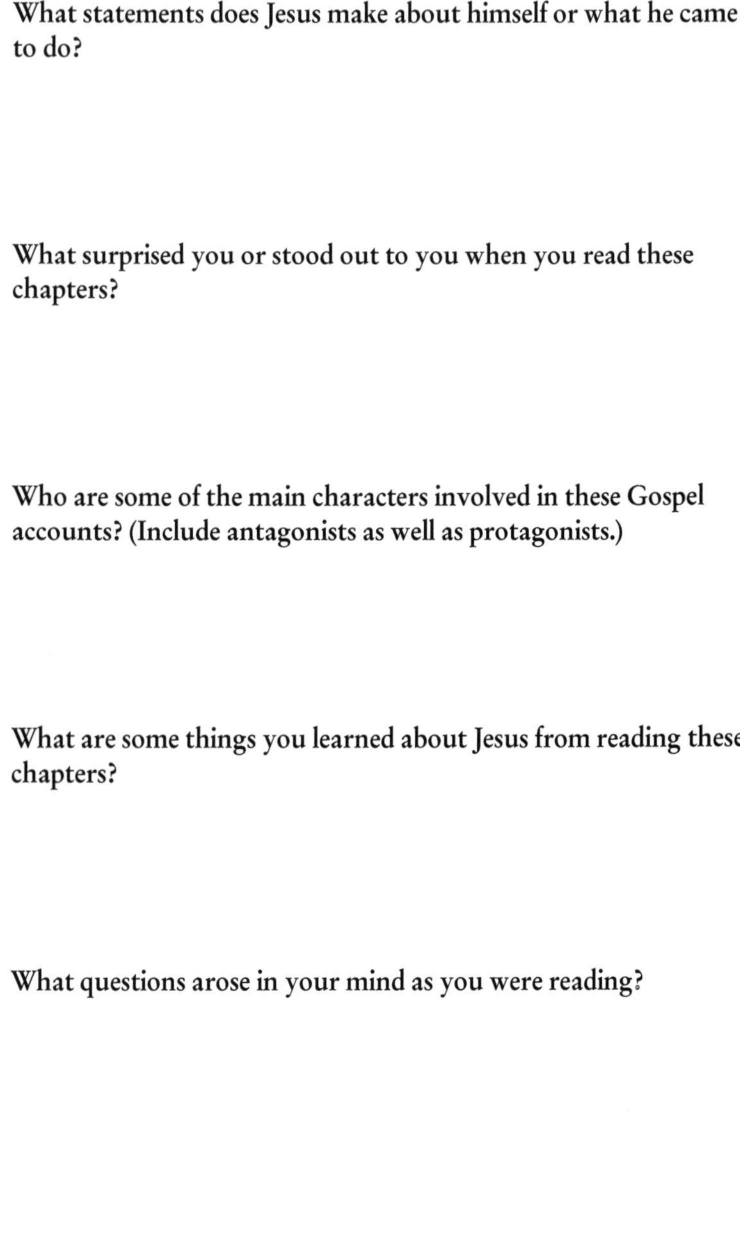

What statements does Jesus make about himself or what he came to do?

What surprised you or stood out to you when you read these chapters?

Who are some of the main characters involved in these Gospel accounts? (Include antagonists as well as protagonists.)

What are some things you learned about Jesus from reading these chapters?

What questions arose in your mind as you were reading?

Day 4

Pray, then read Mark chapters 13–16.

What are some things that Jesus does in these chapters?

What statements does Jesus make about himself or what he came to do?

What surprised you or stood out to you in these chapters?

Who are some of the main characters involved in these Gospel accounts? (Include antagonists as well as protagonists.)

What are some things you learned about Jesus from these chapters?

What questions arose in your mind as you were reading?

Day 5

Remember:

Observation: Figure out what the text is saying. Get the answer from the words of Scripture.

Interpretation: Figure out the meaning of the text. What did the writer intend to convey?

Application: Prayerfully apply the passage to your own life. The application should flow from the interpretation of the text.

Pray, then read Mark 1:1.

1. About whom is Mark writing?

2. The word *gospel* means "good news." Read Isaiah 52:7–10. (See also Isaiah 40:9–11 and Nahum 1:15–2:2.) What would Jews or Gentiles who were familiar with the Old Testament think upon reading this term in Mark?

3. What does the passage in Isaiah tell us about the nature of the good news? (What is the feel or tone of the passage?)

4. If you believe this is joyful news, how should that affect the way you share it?

5. Why do you think Mark introduces his Gospel account with the same words that introduce the creation account in Genesis, i.e., "The beginning"? What is Mark signaling about God and this gospel?

6. *Christ* means "the anointed one." The Jews were waiting for the Christ or Messiah to come in power to rescue Israel and rule over them forever. Read Mark 14:61–62. Jesus tells the high priest that he is the Christ. What else does he say about himself, and what does it mean that the Christ will be seated at the right hand of Power and will come on the clouds of heaven?

7. What does Mark claim about Jesus at the end of verse 1?

8. Read Mark 15:39. What does the centurion say about Jesus?

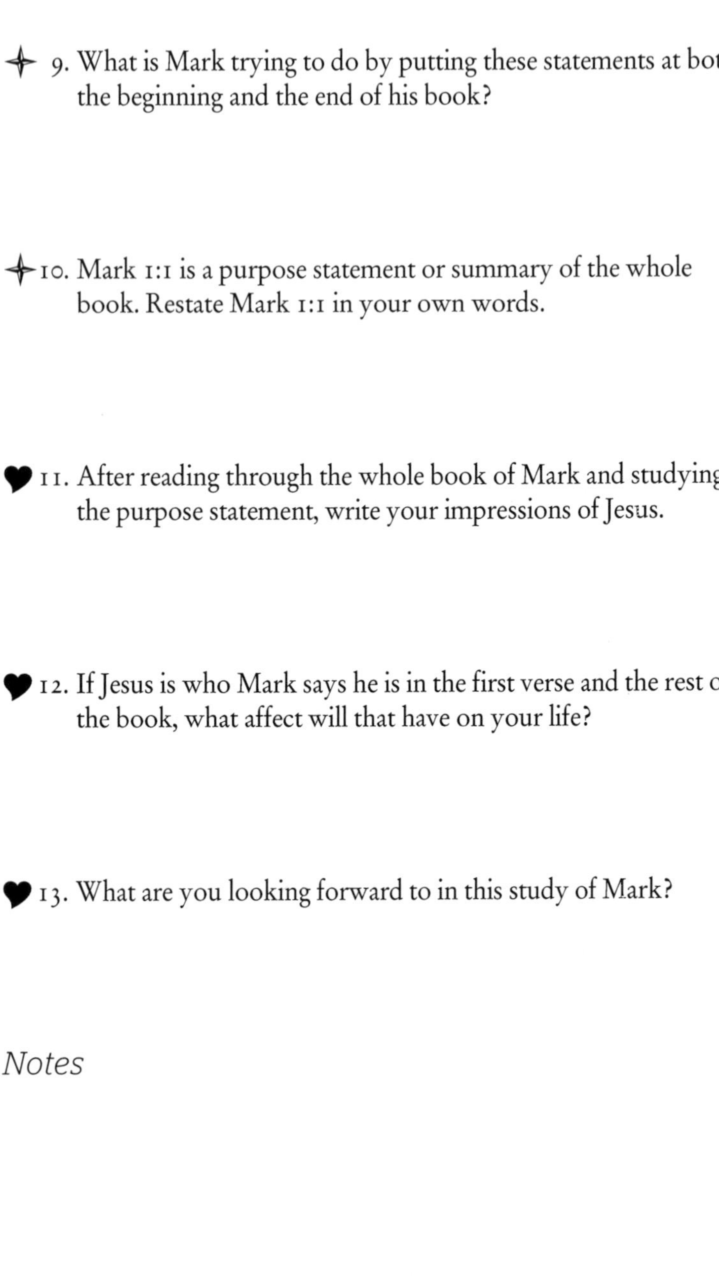

✦ 9. What is Mark trying to do by putting these statements at both the beginning and the end of his book?

✦ 10. Mark 1:1 is a purpose statement or summary of the whole book. Restate Mark 1:1 in your own words.

♥ 11. After reading through the whole book of Mark and studying the purpose statement, write your impressions of Jesus.

♥ 12. If Jesus is who Mark says he is in the first verse and the rest of the book, what affect will that have on your life?

♥ 13. What are you looking forward to in this study of Mark?

Notes

Week 2

Day 1 **Mark 1:1–15**

Begin each day by asking God to open your eyes wider to the true identity of Jesus and the implications of his identity on your life.

Pray, then read Mark 1:1–15.

Mark 1:2–7.

1. To what authority does Mark appeal in verse 2?

2. The words quoted from the Old Testament in verses 2–3 are actually from Malachi as well as Isaiah. (Isaiah is the more prominent prophet and is the lengthier quote.) To understand the context, read Malachi 3:1–5 and Isaiah 40:1–5.

3. Looking at the quote in Mark, who is sending the messenger?

4. What is the messenger to do?

5. Who is coming?

6. Who is Mark announcing as this messenger?

7. What is John doing?

8. What was John's baptism for, and what were the people doing at their baptism?

9. What was John wearing and what did he eat?

10. Read 2 Kings 1:8 and Malachi 4:5–6. What is the symbolism of what John was wearing?

11. Where would John have gotten the food he was eating? What does this tell us about John?

12. How does John's preaching about repentance and the forgiveness of sin correspond to the Old Testament prophecies that Mark quotes? How is the way prepared for the Lord?

13. What does John tell the people about the one who comes after him?

✦ 14. In first century Palestine, untying the straps of sandals was reserved for the lowest, non-Jewish servant. What is John conveying about the one who comes after him when he says he is unworthy of even that service for him?

✦ 15. How does this statement of John the Baptist correspond with the prophecies Mark has quoted?

✦ 16. What does the ministry of John the Baptist tell us about the importance of repentance?

♥ 17. How important is repentance in your life? Do you seek to root out sin in your heart and ask God to give you the gift of repentance? Do you regularly confess your sins to God?

18. What is your view of God? He is both a friend to sinners and so good and holy that he cannot abide sin. How does your life show an awareness of the mighty holiness of God?

Day 2

Pray, then read Mark 1:1–15.

Mark 1:8–11.

1. What will the one who comes after John do?

2. Read Isaiah 44:3–5, Ezekiel 11:17–20, Jeremiah 31:33–34, and Joel 2:28–29. Who sends the Spirit, and what is his role?

3. Based on the Old Testament passages above, what does John mean by Jesus baptizing with the Holy Spirit? What would John's reference to the baptism of the Holy Spirit have signaled to the Jews to whom John was speaking?

4. What does this baptism have to do with John's declaration that the one who comes after him is mightier than he?

5. Every person who has repented of her sin and believed on Jesus has been baptized with the Holy Spirit (See Romans 8:9–11 and 1 Corinthians 12:13). Have you been baptized with the Holy Spirit? What in your life would you point to as evidence that the Holy Spirit is working in you?

6. If you have not been baptized with the Holy Spirit (i.e., if you have not yet repented and believed on Jesus), talk with someone else in your Bible study about why you should believe the gospel of Jesus Christ.

7. Who comes to John to be baptized, and where is he from?

8. John's baptism is for repentance and the forgiveness of sins, but Jesus never sinned. Why would he be baptized? Read Matthew 3:13–15. See 2 Corinthians 5:21 and Hebrews 2:14–18.

9. What surprising things happen after Jesus' baptism while he is still in the water?

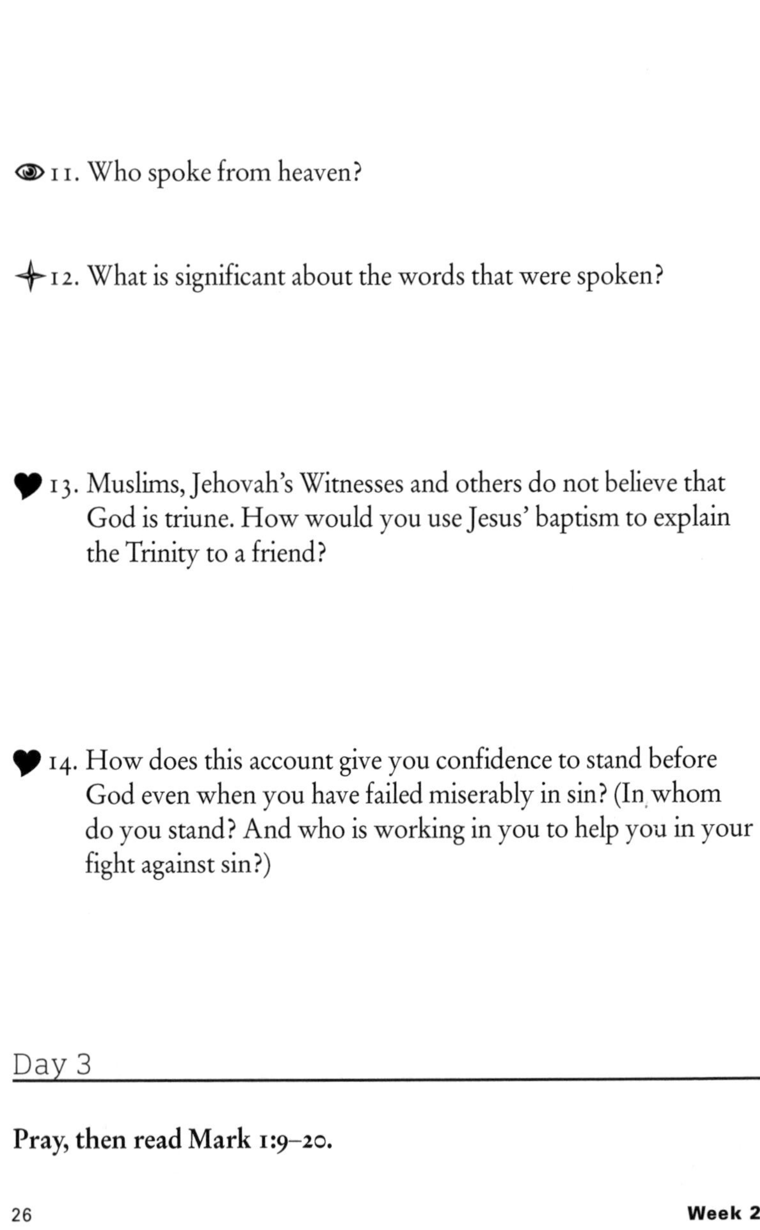

10. What is the significance of the Holy Spirit descending on Jesus? (John 1:32 adds that the Holy Spirit remained on Jesus.)

11. Who spoke from heaven?

12. What is significant about the words that were spoken?

13. Muslims, Jehovah's Witnesses and others do not believe that God is triune. How would you use Jesus' baptism to explain the Trinity to a friend?

14. How does this account give you confidence to stand before God even when you have failed miserably in sin? (In whom do you stand? And who is working in you to help you in your fight against sin?)

Day 3

Pray, then read Mark 1:9–20.

Mark 1:12–13.

1. What does the Spirit do after Jesus' baptism?

2. What happens in the wilderness and for how long?

3. What does verse 13 say Jesus was with in the wilderness?

4. Who was ministering to Jesus?

5. Why is it significant that the Spirit drove Jesus out into the wilderness?

6. What is the significance of Jesus being 40 days in the wilderness? Read Deuteronomy 8:2, Exodus 34:28, and 1 Kings 19:4–8.

7. Read Hebrews 2:14–18 again along with Hebrews 4:15–16. Why was it important for Jesus to suffer the temptations of Satan?

✦ 8. Did Jesus ever give in to temptations?

♥ 9. How does Jesus' sympathy with your weakness help you when you are being tempted?

✦ 10. Notice there are two opposing sides in this struggle. Who is there for Jesus, and who ultimately wins the battle?

♥ 11. Christians suffered much persecution in the first and second centuries. In fact, some were literally being thrown to wild animals. How would this account of Jesus give those Christians comfort?

♥ 12. How can these words comfort you when you are facing persecution or trials?

Day 4

Pray, then read Mark 1:9–20.

Mark 1:14–15

1. What happened to John?

2. Where did Jesus go, and what did he proclaim? (See also Isaiah 9:1–4.)

3. What does Jesus mean when he says, "The time is fulfilled"? See Galatians 4:4–5 and Ephesians 1:7–10.

4. What is the kingdom of God?

5. What response to the kingdom does Jesus call for?

6. What is the gospel that Jesus proclaimed? (What was Jesus urging people to believe?)

✦ 7. What does it mean to repent?

♥ 8. Have you repented and believed the gospel? If not, why not? If so, briefly describe the circumstances.

♥ 9. If you haven't believed the gospel, take some time to pray that God would open your eyes to his truth. If you have believed, take some time to praise God for opening your eyes to the truth of the gospel.

Day 5

Pray, then read Mark 1:1–15.

Mark often uses a literary devise called an "inclusio," sometimes called "top and tail," to make his main points. An inclusio is where the writer states a theme or main idea at the beginning (top) and ending (tail) of a portion of text. The material in between the statements are related to the main idea. (Mark 1:1 and 15:39 are inclusios for the entire Gospel.)

✦ 1. Last week, we discovered that Mark 1:1 was a purpose statement for the Gospel of Mark. Rewrite your restatement of Mark 1:1 from Day 5, question 10.

✦ 2. How are verses 14–15 related to verse 1? Point out all the parallels.

✦ 3. There are three closely related themes in verses 1 and 14–15: the gospel, Jesus is the Christ, and Jesus is the Son of God. Considering all you've studied this week, how do these three themes come through in verses 2–13?

✦ The Gospel:

✦ Jesus is the Christ:

✦ Jesus is the Son of God:

♥ 4. What is the application for your life in each of these areas?

- ♥ The Gospel:

- ♥ Jesus is the Christ:

- ♥ Jesus is the Son of God:

Notes

Week 3

Day 1 **Mark 1:16-39**

Begin each day by praying that you would be newly amazed by Jesus.

Pray, then read Mark 1:14–20.

Mark 1:16–20

1. What does Jesus see Simon and his brother Andrew doing?

2. What does Jesus tell them to do?

3. How do they respond to Jesus?

4. What does Jesus see James and John doing, and what does he say to them?

5. How do they respond to Jesus?

6. What does Jesus mean when he says, "I will make you fishers of men"? For what purpose has he called these men?

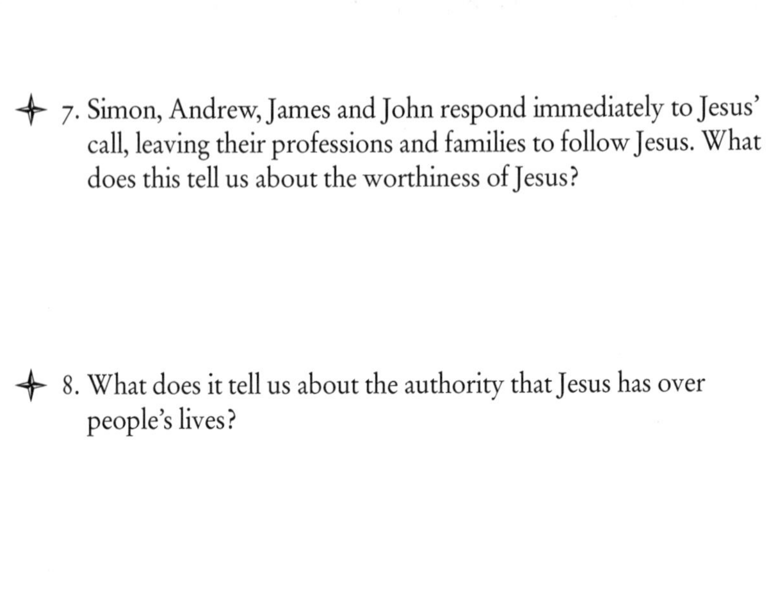

7. Simon, Andrew, James and John respond immediately to Jesus' call, leaving their professions and families to follow Jesus. What does this tell us about the worthiness of Jesus?

8. What does it tell us about the authority that Jesus has over people's lives?

9. Do you see the supreme worthiness of Jesus? What have you left or given up to follow him?

10. What in your life shows that Jesus is your ultimate authority?

11. Jesus calls all his disciples to be "fishers of men." (See Matthew 28:18–20.) Are you a fisher of men? What has been your experience with evangelism?

♥ 12. As you think back over what you've studied this week, what stands out to you about Jesus? And what does that tell you about how you should relate to him?

Day 2

Pray, then read Mark 1:16–28.

Mark 1:21–28

✦ 1. Who went to Capernaum? (Who is the "they"?)

◉ 2. What does Jesus do in the synagogue? (Synagogues are Jewish places of teaching and worship.)

◉ 3. How do the people respond to Jesus' teaching, and why?

✦ 4. Scribes were respected Jewish teachers who interpreted the Law to the people. They knew rabbinic teaching well and referred to it as the authority for their interpretations of the Law. What did it mean for Jesus to "teach as one who had authority, and not as the scribes"? What was the difference between Jesus' teaching and the scribes' teaching?

5. What does the unclean spirit assume Jesus has come to do?

6. What does the unclean spirit know about Jesus?

7. How does Jesus rebuke him?

8. What happens when Jesus tells the spirit to come out of the man?

9. How do the people respond, and how do they describe Jesus' teaching?

10. What was "new" about Jesus teaching?

11. How does Jesus casting out the demon further reinforce the authority with which he teaches?

12. Where do we find Jesus' teaching today? What does this tell us about the authority of the Bible?

Day 3

Pray, then read Mark 1:16–28.

Mark 1:21–28

1. Review your notes from yesterday's study of Mark 1:21–28.

2. In verses 16–20, we saw Jesus has authority over people. Over what two things does Jesus show his authority in verses 21–28?

3. How does this authority give evidence to Mark's statement in verse 1 that Jesus is the Son of God?

4. What happens in verse 28 as a result of Jesus casting out this demon?

5. How does knowing Jesus' absolute power over demons give you confidence when you think about the forces of evil?

6. How does Jesus' power give you confidence when fighting your own sin?

7. How do you use Jesus' teaching to fight the devil and sin?

Day 4

Pray, then read Mark 1:21–39.

Mark 1:29–34

1. Where does Jesus go and with whom?

2. Who is ill?

3. What does Jesus do?

4. How does Simon's mother-in-law respond?

5. What stands out to you in this account of Jesus healing Simon's mother-in-law?

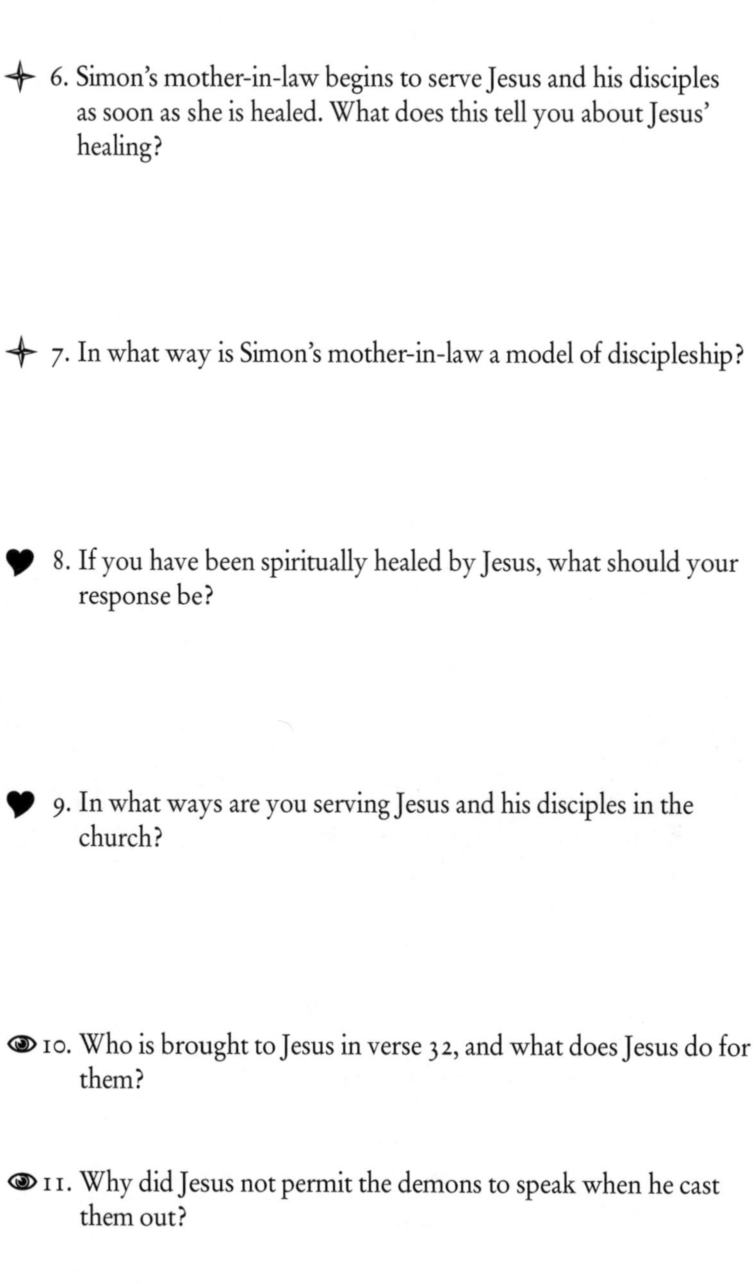

6. Simon's mother-in-law begins to serve Jesus and his disciples as soon as she is healed. What does this tell you about Jesus' healing?

7. In what way is Simon's mother-in-law a model of discipleship?

8. If you have been spiritually healed by Jesus, what should your response be?

9. In what ways are you serving Jesus and his disciples in the church?

10. Who is brought to Jesus in verse 32, and what does Jesus do for them?

11. Why did Jesus not permit the demons to speak when he cast them out?

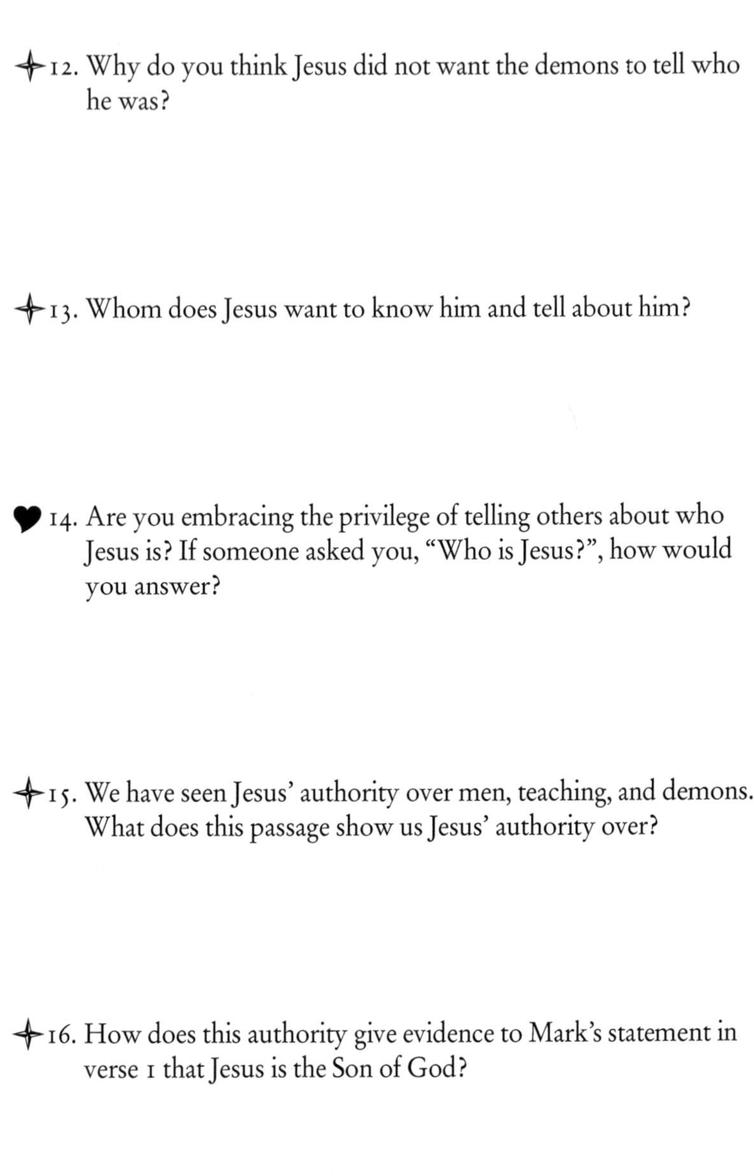

12. Why do you think Jesus did not want the demons to tell who he was?

13. Whom does Jesus want to know him and tell about him?

14. Are you embracing the privilege of telling others about who Jesus is? If someone asked you, "Who is Jesus?", how would you answer?

15. We have seen Jesus' authority over men, teaching, and demons. What does this passage show us Jesus' authority over?

16. How does this authority give evidence to Mark's statement in verse 1 that Jesus is the Son of God?

17. If you have put your trust in Jesus, how does his authority over sickness give you hope when you are suffering with sickness or physical pain, even though we know from other passages of Scripture that we will not always be healthy or receive healing? (See also John 16:33.)

18. How can you encourage other believers who are going through physical trials?

Day 5

Pray, then read Mark 1:29–45.

Mark 1:35–39

1. What does Jesus do very early in the morning?

2. What do Simon and those who are with him do?

3. What do you think Simon and the other disciples expect of Jesus?

4. What does Jesus tell the disciples they are going?

5. Why did Jesus come out?

6. What does Jesus then do throughout all Galilee?

7. What are Jesus' clear priorities shown in this passage?

8. What does Jesus' prayer life tell us about his relationship with God the Father?

9. If Jesus, the Son of God, needs to pray, how much more do we need it? How would you describe your prayer life?

10. How would you like your prayer life to change?

✦ 11. We see in verses 28, 33, and 37 that Jesus' fame is spreading. Jesus is drawing large crowds who want things from him, but he does not allow crowds or even his disciples to set his priorities. He has a plan and will carry it out. What does this tell you about Jesus?

♥ 12. Do your priorities line up with Jesus? Explain how they do or how they don't:

♥ 13. What tends to sidetrack you and cause you to forget about the priority of Jesus' teaching and your proclaiming the gospel?

♥ 14. What can you do to persevere in the priorities that Jesus would have for you?

Notes

Week 4

Day 1 **Mark 1:40–2:28**

Begin each day praying that you would understand what it means for Jesus to have come to call not the righteous, but sinners to himself.

Pray, then read Mark 1:35–45.

Mark 1:40–45

1. Who comes to Jesus, and what does he say?

2. Leprous disease made one unclean according to the law (see Leviticus 13). The person with leprosy would have to live separately from the community of Israel and would be prohibited from worshipping the Lord in the temple. Why do you think the man with leprosy asked to be made "clean" rather than healed?

3. What does the man's statement tell you about what he believes about Jesus?

4. What does Jesus feel, do, and say in response to the man's plea?

5. Why is it surprising that Jesus touched this man?

6. What is the result of Jesus' touch and word?

7. Jesus was moved with pity for this man, desired to make him clean and willingly touched him. What do these things tell you about Jesus?

8. Is Jesus where you go when you are desperate and unclean? Do you know that he moves toward sinners and desires to make you clean? How does this affect your life?

9. Have you experienced the compassion and deep love of Jesus? What difference does it make in your life?

10. What does Jesus tell the now clean man to do? (See Leviticus 14 for laws on cleansing lepers.)

11. How does the man respond, and what is the result?

12. Why do you think Jesus told the man not to talk to anyone?

13. Why do you think the man spread the news of his healing even though Jesus told him not to?

14. If you have been "made clean" by Jesus, are you like this man, spreading the news? Why, or why not?

Day 2

Pray, then read Mark 1:40–2:12.

Mark 2:1–12

1. What happens when Jesus returns home?

2. What is Jesus doing?

3. What do the four men do to get the paralytic in front of Jesus?

4. What does this tell you about the four men's attitudes toward the paralytic and toward Jesus?

5. What does Jesus see in this act, and what does he say?

6. How do the scribes respond to Jesus' statement?

7. Why do the scribes think that Jesus' pronouncement of forgiveness is blasphemy? Who can forgive sins but God alone? (See also Psalms 51:1–4.)

8. Why do you think Jesus pronounces forgiveness on the paralytic as opposed to the four men who lowered him into the room?

9. What does Jesus perceive about the scribes and how does he challenge their questioning?

10. What happens when Jesus tells the paralytic to "rise, pick up your bed, and go home"?

11. Why does Jesus heal the paralytic?

12. How is this healing evidence that Jesus has the authority to forgive sins?

13. Jesus refers to himself as the Son of Man. His hearers would have thought that he was either calling himself a mortal man as in Ezekiel 2:7 or that he was referring to himself as the Son of Man in Daniel 7:13 who comes as God's representative and rules forever. What do you think Jesus meant in using that title here?

14. How does the gathered crowd respond to the healing of the paralytic?

15. Jesus is in a crowded house preaching the word. He does not automatically heal the paralytic but first declares his sins forgiven. What does this tell you about Jesus' priorities?

✦ 16. What does this account tell you about the purpose behind Jesus' miracles?

♥ 17. Jesus forgives sin! Are you aware of the sin in your life? How regularly do you go to God with your sin and find forgiveness through Jesus?

♥ 18. How can this account help shape your priorities in prayer for yourself and others?

♥ 19. This week we have read about Jesus healing Simon's mother-in-law, a leper, and a paralytic. What stands out most to you about Jesus in these historical accounts? Take some time to glorify God for these things.

Day 3

Read Mark 2:1–17.

Mark 2:13–17

1. Who was coming to Jesus, and what was he doing?

2. Who does Jesus see, and what does he say to him?

3. Where was Levi sitting, and how does he respond to Jesus' call?

4. Who was reclining with Jesus and his disciples in Levi's house?

5. What do the scribes of the Pharisees question Jesus' disciples about?

6. Tax collectors were Jews who worked with Roman authorities to collect taxes from fellow Jews. They would make money by charging their compatriots more than they actually owed. Why would it have been shocking for a religious teacher like Jesus to choose a tax collector to be his close disciple and to eat with tax collectors and sinners?

7. How does Jesus respond to the Pharisees?

8. Jesus lived a life without sin and called others to repent of their sin, even telling them to cut off the hand or foot or gouge

out the eye that causes them to sin (Mark 9:43–48). Is Jesus condoning the sin of these tax collectors and sinners? Explain.

✦ 9. What does Jesus mean when he says, "Those who are well have no need of a physician, but those who are sick"?

✦ 10. Why do you think Mark puts this account right after the account of the paralytic?

♥ 11. There's an old hymn that says, "Come ye sinners, poor and wretched, weak and wounded, sick and sore; Jesus ready, stands to save you, full of pity, joined with power ... Let not conscience make you linger, nor of fitness fondly dream; All the fitness he requires is to feel your need of him." Do you feel your need of him? Examine your heart to see if there is some "righteousness" like that of the Pharisees, that holds you back from fully relying on Jesus.

♥ 12. Verse 15 says that "many tax collectors and sinners" were following Jesus. What is your attitude toward other people?

Do you regard some as too sinful to come to Jesus or not the right type of person? Which sinners are you reaching out to?

13. What about you? Do you see yourself as too sinful to come to Jesus? Do you think you have to clean up your life first? What does this passage tell you?

Day 4

Pray, then read Mark 2:15–28.

Mark 2:18–22.

1. What were John the Baptist's disciples and the Pharisees doing, and what do the people ask Jesus?

2. In his answer, to whom does Jesus compare himself?

3. What do wedding guests do as opposed to fasting?

4. How does this relate to the text we studied yesterday?

5. What does Jesus say will happen to the bridegroom, and how will the disciples respond then?

6. What is Jesus alluding to when he says the bridegroom will be taken away?

7. As Christians, we live in the already-not yet of the kingdom of God. The bridegroom has already come and is with us by his Spirit, but he will come again in power and usher us fully into his everlasting kingdom. Should we be rejoicing with the bridegroom or fasting while we await his return, or both? Explain your answer.

8. What two examples or pictures does Jesus use next to explain why his disciples are different?

9. What do the old garment and the old wineskins represent in this context?

✦ 10. What do the new cloth and the new wine represent?

✦ 11. What happens when one tries to force the new onto the old?

✦ 12. Notice the destruction that occurs when the new is forced into the old. What is Jesus saying by using these examples?

♥ 13. What would you say to a friend who wanted to follow Jesus but felt she needed to also follow certain ceremonial laws to be right with God?

♥ 14. What about a Muslim friend who wants to continue fasting and ritual prayers at the mosque while following Jesus?

♥ 15. Are there ways that you have added Jesus onto your old life instead of centering your life on him? What can you do to prevent the tearing and bursting that are bound to occur?

Day 5

Pray, then read Mark 2:15–28.

Mark 2:23–28

1. What were the disciples doing on the Sabbath?

2. What do the Pharisees say about it?

3. To which Old Testament account does Jesus point to justify the actions of his disciples?

4. What does Jesus say about the Sabbath?

5. Explain how the Sabbath is for man. See Genesis 2:1–3 and Exodus 20:1–2, 8–11.

6. What does Jesus say about the Son of Man and the Sabbath?

✦ 7. Read 1 Samuel 21:1–6. David is running from Saul the king and eats bread that was only lawfully eaten by priests. Scripture does not record any reproof of David for this action. What point is Jesus making, using the account about David?

✦ 8. What is Jesus saying about his relationship to the Sabbath, particularly in verse 28?

✦ 9. If Jesus is Lord of the Sabbath, what does this say about who he is and his ability to interpret the law?

♥ 10. After Jesus' resurrection, Christians began to meet together on Sundays instead of Saturdays (the Sabbath), calling Sundays, the Lord's Day. What does this passage tell you about who should be the center of the Lord's Day (and every other day of the week)?

♥ 11. How can you make Jesus more central when you gather with the saints?

Notes

Week 5

Day 1 **Mark 3**

Pray to see wondrous things about Jesus this week and ask God to show you how to follow him more closely.

Pray, then read Mark 3.

1. Where does Jesus go, and who is there?

2. Who is watching Jesus, and why?

3. What does Jesus ask the Pharisees, and how do they respond?

4. How does Jesus feel about the Pharisees attitude toward the man with the withered hand?

5. What does Jesus say to the man, and what happens?

6. What is the Pharisees' response to Jesus healing the man?

7. What are the Pharisees elevating the Sabbath over in their legalism?

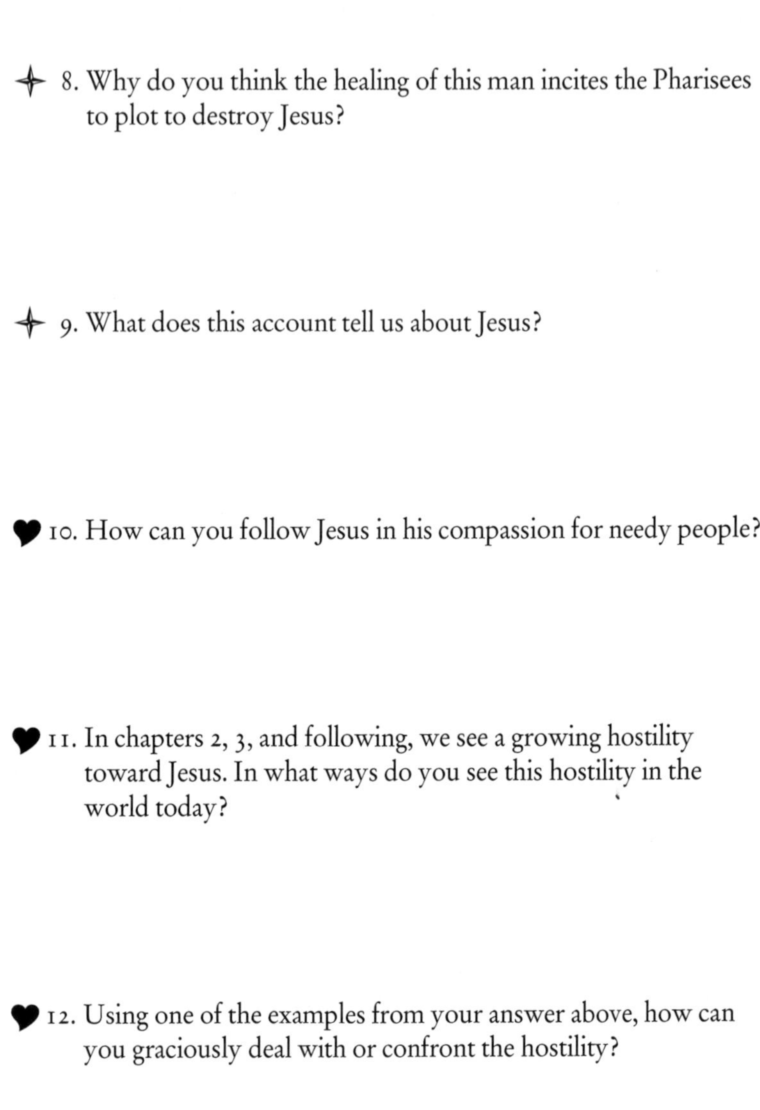

8. Why do you think the healing of this man incites the Pharisees to plot to destroy Jesus?

9. What does this account tell us about Jesus?

10. How can you follow Jesus in his compassion for needy people?

11. In chapters 2, 3, and following, we see a growing hostility toward Jesus. In what ways do you see this hostility in the world today?

12. Using one of the examples from your answer above, how can you graciously deal with or confront the hostility?

Day 2

Pray, then read Mark 3:1–21.

Mark 3:7–12

1. What happens when Jesus withdraws with his disciples?

2. Why does the "great crowd" come to Jesus?

3. Why does Jesus have a boat prepared?

4. How does the crowd's reaction to Jesus compare to the Pharisees' reaction that we have seen in previous passages?

5. How do the unclean spirits react when they see Jesus?

6. What does Jesus order the unclean spirits?

7. Mark seems to emphasize Jesus' casting out of demons. What is Mark showing his readers?

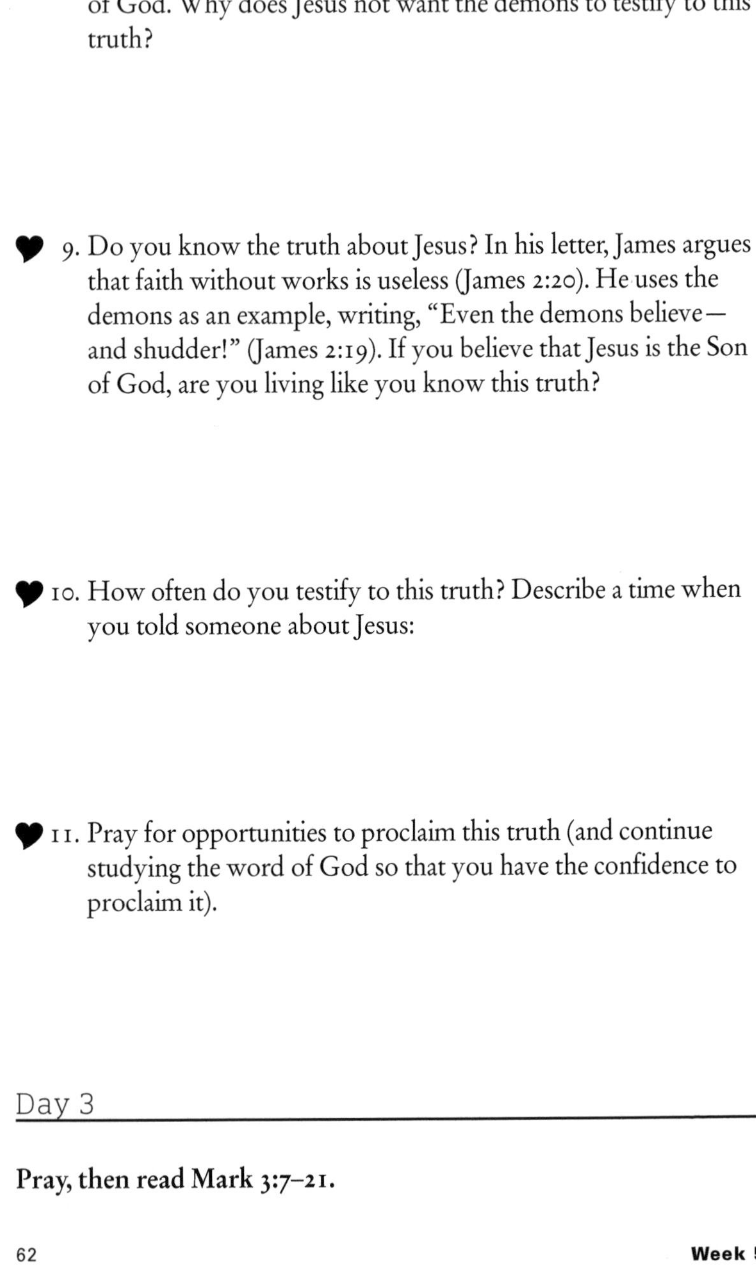

8. The demons know the truth about Jesus—that he is the Son of God. Why does Jesus not want the demons to testify to this truth?

9. Do you know the truth about Jesus? In his letter, James argues that faith without works is useless (James 2:20). He uses the demons as an example, writing, "Even the demons believe—and shudder!" (James 2:19). If you believe that Jesus is the Son of God, are you living like you know this truth?

10. How often do you testify to this truth? Describe a time when you told someone about Jesus:

11. Pray for opportunities to proclaim this truth (and continue studying the word of God so that you have the confidence to proclaim it).

Day 3

Pray, then read Mark 3:7–21.

Mark 3:13–19

1. Where did Jesus go, and what did he do?

2. For what purpose did he appoint the twelve men?

3. Read Acts 1:15–22. In appointing an apostle to replace Judas, what did the other apostles look for?

4. What was this replacement joining the other apostles to do?

5. Read Acts 1:23–26. How was Matthias chosen? Who ultimately chose him?

6. Read John 15:26–27. In John 15, Jesus is speaking to the disciples after Judas has left them. What does Jesus tell the disciples they will do, and how are they uniquely qualified for this task?

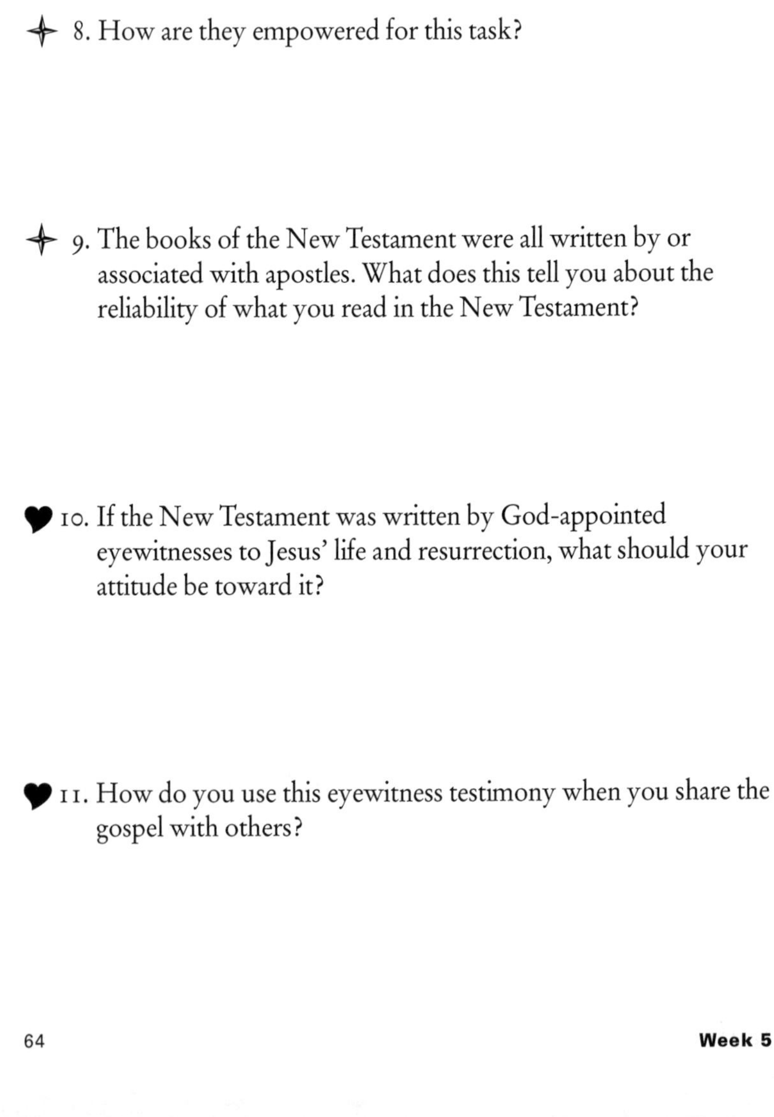

7. Thinking about these passages in Mark, Acts, and John together, who chooses apostles? What must they have witnessed? And what is their unique task?

8. How are they empowered for this task?

9. The books of the New Testament were all written by or associated with apostles. What does this tell you about the reliability of what you read in the New Testament?

10. If the New Testament was written by God-appointed eyewitnesses to Jesus' life and resurrection, what should your attitude be toward it?

11. How do you use this eyewitness testimony when you share the gospel with others?

12. In the Old Testament, the people of God came from the twelve heads of the tribes of Israel—the sons of Jacob. What does this have to do with the twelve apostles? See Revelation 21:10–14.

13. If the foundation of the church is the apostles teaching (see Ephesians 2:20), what does that tell us about the place of the Scriptures in our local church? What are the characteristics of a church centered on the teaching of the apostles?

14. What does Mark mention about Judas at the end of the list of apostles?

15. What can you infer about Jesus and his mission from the fact that he chose someone to be with him in his inner circle who would betray him?

Mark 3:20–21

16. Where does Jesus go, and what happens again?

17. How does Jesus' family respond?

18. Jesus' family had watched him grow up without sin. They should have known him intimately. How can their response be explained?

19. How does this account serve as a warning for those of us who are regular church-goers or have grown up in a Christian family?

Day 4

Pray, then read Mark 3:13–35.

Mark 3:22–27

1. Who came down from Jerusalem, and what did they say?

2. What is the first parable Jesus uses to respond to the scribes' accusations?

3. What is the point of the parable?

4. What is the second parable Jesus uses?

5. Whom does the strong man represent? What do his house and goods represent?

6. How is someone able to plunder his house?

7. Thinking back over the first three chapters of Mark, how has Jesus shown that he has bound the strong man and is plundering his house?

8. How does the fact that Jesus is infinitely stronger than the strong man help you when you face difficulty in life?

9. How does this knowledge help you fight sin?

Mark 3:28–30

10. What sin does Jesus say will be forgiven; and, conversely, what is an eternal sin that cannot be forgiven?

11. Why does Jesus give this warning to the scribes?

12. About whom does the Holy Spirit testify? And about whom do the Pharisees accuse of having an unclean spirit?

13. Jesus welcomed tax collectors and sinners. So what does it mean to commit this eternal sin that cannot be forgiven? How does verse 30 shed light on this "unpardonable sin"?

14. Verses 29–30 are some of the most difficult verses in the Bible to interpret and apply. In his *Systematic Theology*, John Frame describes the unpardonable sin as "malicious, willful rejection and slander against the Holy Spirit's work attesting to God, and attributing that work to Satan" (p. 851). Do you fear you have blasphemed against the Holy Spirit? If so, the fear itself is evidence that you probably have not. Talk to your pastor or another trusted church leader about your concerns.

Day 5

Pray, then read Mark 3:20–35.

Mark 3:31–34

1. Remembering verse 21, what are Jesus' mother and brothers trying to do?

2. When the crowd tells Jesus his mother and brothers are seeking him, who does Jesus declare to be his mother, sisters and brothers?

3. What point is Jesus making about who he is, and who his true family is?

4. Is an intellectual knowledge of Jesus enough for a relationship with him? What distinguishes between Jesus' true followers and those who just claim to know him?

♥ 5. If we are following Jesus, who are our true brothers and sisters? What do these verses suggest about our relationships in our local church?

♥ 6. Do you consider your fellow church members to be your family? How can you cultivate deeper relationships with others in your church?

Notes

Week 6

Day 1 — Mark 4:1-34

This week pray for deeper understanding of the kingdom of God and a stronger desire for it to grow.

Pray, then read Mark 4:1–34.

Mark 4:1–8 and 14–20

1. What is Jesus doing, and where is he doing it?

2. Who is Jesus teaching, and what is he using to teach?

3. Who is the main actor in the parable, and what is he doing?

4. Fill in the first two boxes for each of the soils in the chart below:

Type of soil	What happens to seed or plant	What soil represents

5. Skip verses 9–13 for now. What does Jesus say the seeds represent? What is the sower sowing?

6. What does Jesus mean by "the word"?

7. Go back to the chart and fill in the last column.

8. Looking at the chart, put the last column for each soil in your own words:

9. Do you know anyone whose heart has been like the path? Describe that person's response to the word:

10. What about the rocky ground? Describe the circumstances of that person's life:

♥ 11. Do you know thorny-soil people? Describe:

✦ 12. What does Jesus mean when he describes the good soil bearing much fruit. What is the fruit?

♥ 11. Now describe someone you know whose heart has produced much fruit:

♥ 14. Shallowness or thorniness: does your heart struggle with either of these things? Do you struggle spiritually when you face difficulties or persecution? Or are you tempted to desire the things of this world more than Christ?

♥ 15. Notice that in each of the first three soils the word dies. How can you till the soil of your heart and make sure to heed Jesus' warning in this parable?

Day 2

Pray, then read Mark 4:1–20.

Mark 4:9–13

1. Jesus has just told people the parable of the soils. What does he urge them after he finishes?

2. He also specifically urges his disciples to "hear" after the next parable he tells (v. 23). Obviously, the people who were listening to Jesus could physically "hear" him. What does it mean to have "ears to hear"?

3. When the disciples are alone with Jesus, what do they ask him about?

4. What does Jesus tell them in verse 11?

5. In what way is the kingdom of God secret?

6. Who are "those outside"?

7. How does Jesus describe the purpose of the parables in verse 12?

8. How would you state this purpose in your own words?

9. Read Isaiah 6:8–13, the passage from which Jesus quotes. Read also Romans 11:7–12 which also quotes from the Old Testament. How do these passages shed light on Jesus' use of parables?

10. Read Deuteronomy 29:4 and 2 Corinthians 3:14. What must happen for people to understand?

11. To whom is Jesus speaking in Mark 4:13, and what is his concern with them?

12. What does Jesus proceed to do in the following verses?

♥ 13. How does the disciples' lack of understanding in this passage give you hope when you read something in the Scriptures that you do not understand?

♥ 14. What is your experience with the word of God? When you study it more and hear it taught do you understand it better and bear more fruit?

♥ 15. What should you do if you have a hardened heart or a lack of understanding?

♥ 16. How does this passage affect your evangelism? What should you do when you come across someone without ears to hear?

Day 3

Pray, then read Mark 4:14–34.

Mark 4:21–25

1. What is the second parable or illustration Jesus uses with his disciples?

2. How does Jesus explain the parable?

3. What does the lamp represent? See Isaiah 9:2 and John 1:1–9.

4. Explain what the lamp will do.

5. How do you feel about your secrets coming to light?

6. What does Jesus urge the disciples in verses 23 and 24?

7. Why should they pay attention?

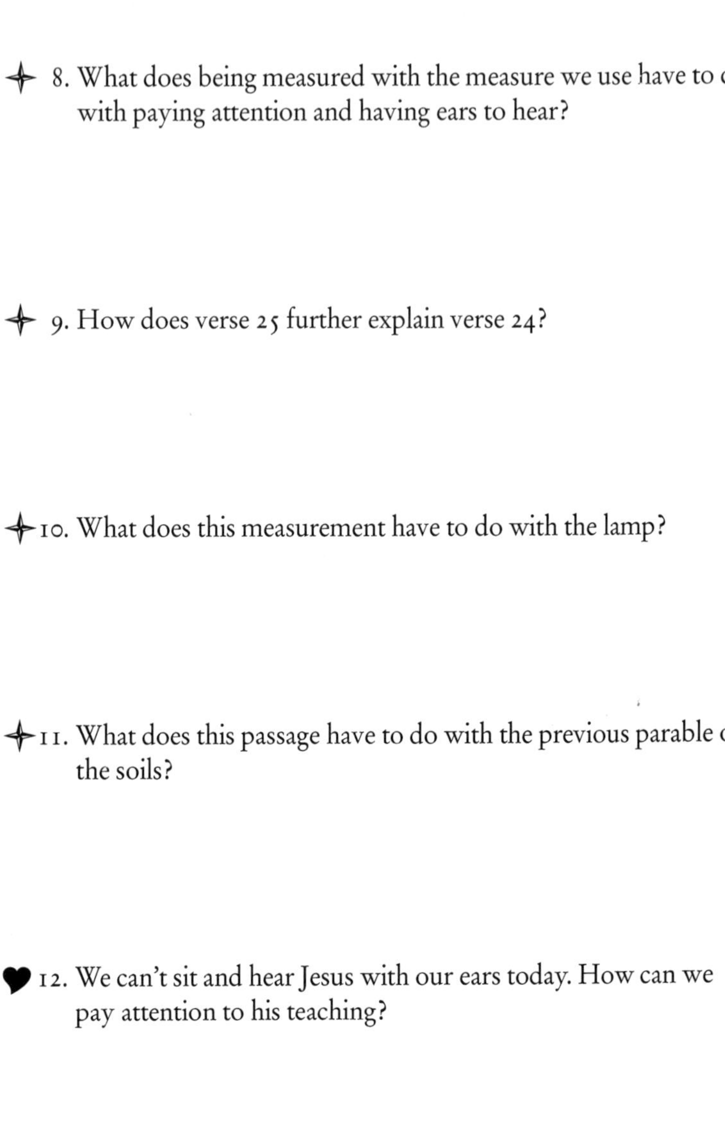

8. What does being measured with the measure we use have to do with paying attention and having ears to hear?

9. How does verse 25 further explain verse 24?

10. What does this measurement have to do with the lamp?

11. What does this passage have to do with the previous parable of the soils?

12. We can't sit and hear Jesus with our ears today. How can we pay attention to his teaching?

♥ 13. Are you attentive to the word of God? How do you benefit from hearing God's word preached on Sundays?

♥ 14. Do you take advantage of other opportunities to hear the word taught: Sunday school, Bible studies, or other church classes? Is learning the Scriptures a priority in your life?

♥ 15. Do you regularly spend personal, private time in the word?

Day 4

Pray, then read Mark 4:21–41.

Mark 4:26–29

👁 1. What does Jesus liken the kingdom of God to in this parable?

👁 2. What does the man do, and what does the seed do?

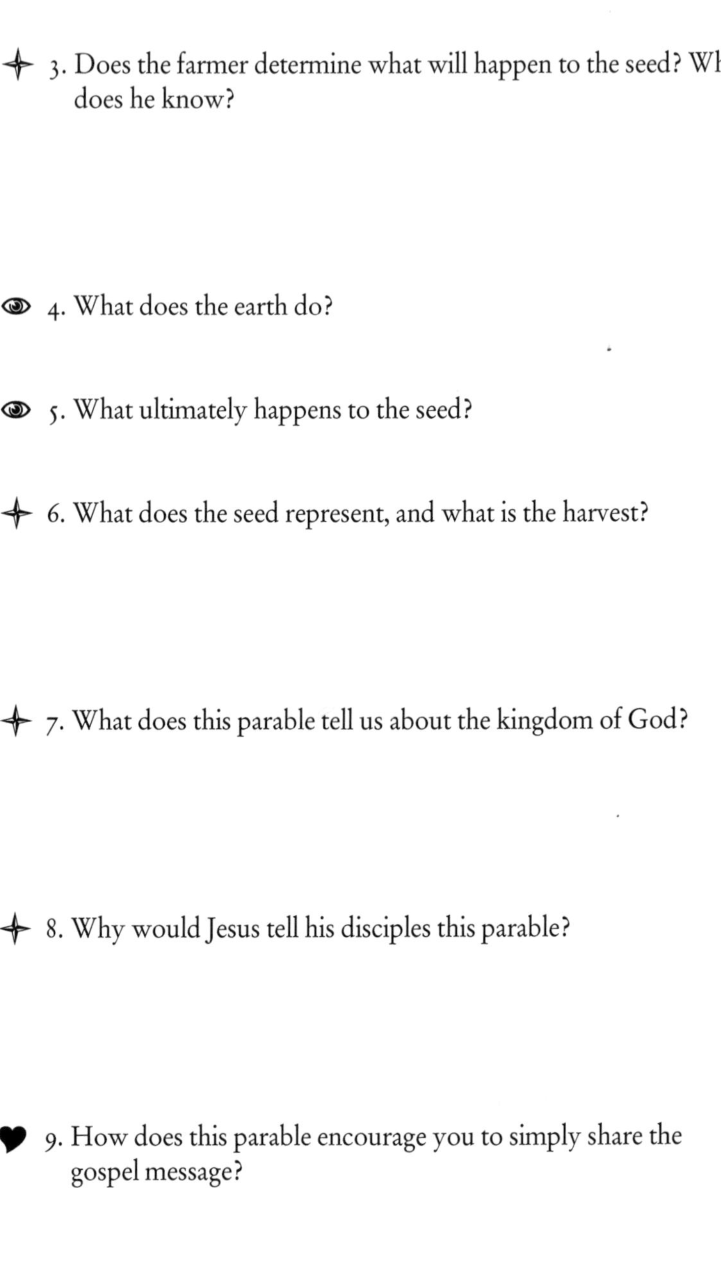

3. Does the farmer determine what will happen to the seed? What does he know?

4. What does the earth do?

5. What ultimately happens to the seed?

6. What does the seed represent, and what is the harvest?

7. What does this parable tell us about the kingdom of God?

8. Why would Jesus tell his disciples this parable?

9. How does this parable encourage you to simply share the gospel message?

♥ 10. How can this parable give you confidence if you don't see immediate fruit from sharing the gospel?

Day 5

Pray, then read Mark 4:26–34.

Mark 4:30–34

1. To what does Jesus compare the kingdom of God in the next parable?

2. What is special about the mustard seed?

3. The mustard seed is not the smallest seed in the world, but it was the smallest seed used by first century Palestinian farmers. Is Jesus making a scientific point in this parable, or is he using everyday language that his hearers would understand? What would you say to someone who argued that Jesus said something false about the mustard seed?

4. What would one expect of the tiny mustard seed before planting?

5. What actually happens to the mustard seed?

6. What point is Jesus making with this parable?

7. To whom does Jesus tell parables, and to whom does he explain the parables?

8. How would this parable have encouraged the 1st century persecuted and scattered church to whom Mark was writing?

9. Describe how you have seen the gospel seed work this way in your life or in your church:

10. How does it give you confidence when you scatter seed and don't see immediate growth?

♥ 11. How does it give you confidence in the gospel seed even if you feel personally inadequate when spreading it?

♥ 12. In this secular age when biblical Christianity is becoming more and more marginalized, how do these two short parables on the kingdom of God give us hope?

Notes

Notes

Week 7

Day 1 **Mark 4:35-5:43**

Pray this week that you would be aware of your uncleanness and even more aware of Jesus' power to make you clean.

Pray, then read Mark 4:21–41.

Mark 4:35–41

✦ 1. What had Jesus been teaching about on "that day"?

👁 2. What does Jesus tell the disciples to do that evening?

👁 3. What happens to the boat?

👁 4. What is Jesus doing while the waves are breaking into the boat and filling it with water?

✦ 5. What does this tell you about Jesus?

👁 6. What do the disciples do?

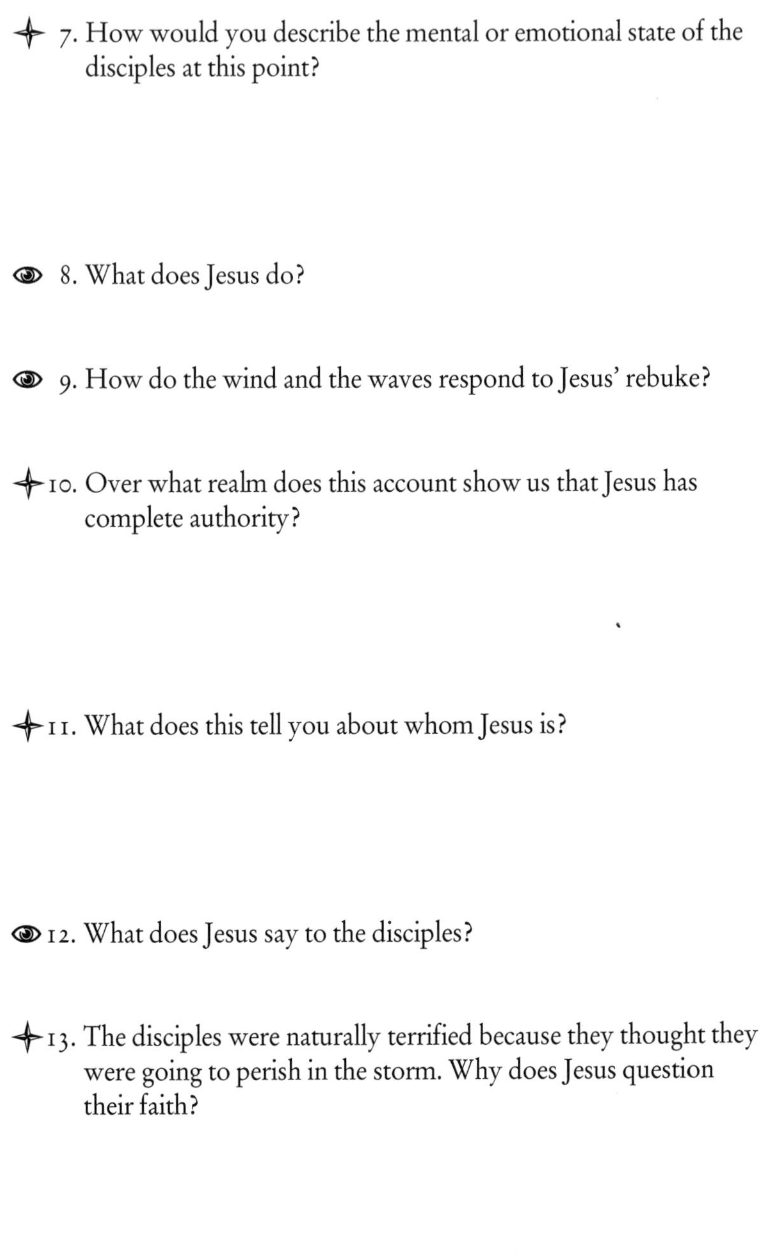

✦ 7. How would you describe the mental or emotional state of the disciples at this point?

👁 8. What does Jesus do?

👁 9. How do the wind and the waves respond to Jesus' rebuke?

✦ 10. Over what realm does this account show us that Jesus has complete authority?

✦ 11. What does this tell you about whom Jesus is?

👁 12. What does Jesus say to the disciples?

✦ 13. The disciples were naturally terrified because they thought they were going to perish in the storm. Why does Jesus question their faith?

14. How do the disciples react to Jesus calming the wind and the waves, and what question do they ask about him?

15. Why is the disciples' response to Jesus one of fear rather than rejoicing, and what does their question have to do with their fear?

16. How would you answer the disciples' question? Explain your answer.

17. How do you react to the storms of life? With fear or calm assurance that Jesus is in control?

18. We have seen that Jesus has authority over men, sickness, the forgiveness of sins, and the spiritual realm. Now we see that he has authority over nature. If you are a Christian, how does Jesus' authority over these things give you comfort and confidence?

19. How does this account of Jesus calming the wind and the waves relate to the parables Jesus told earlier in the day?

20. How does the knowledge that Jesus is the King of the kingdom of God help you cultivate calm assurance during the storms of life?

Day 2

Pray, then read Mark 4:35–5:20.

Mark 5:1–20

1. Describe the man who meets Jesus when he steps out of the boat on the other side of the sea:

2. What has the unclean spirit done to the man?

3. What does the man do when he sees Jesus?

4. What does Jesus say to the unclean spirit?

5. How does the unclean spirit respond?

6. What is the name of the unclean spirit?

(Note: A legion was a large company of Roman soldiers numbering up to 6,000. [*ESV Study Bible* note on Mark 5:9.])

7. What does the unclean spirit ask of Jesus?

8. How does Jesus respond to this request, and what happens?

9. Why do you think Jesus grants the request of the evil spirit? What does it confirm about the demons? What does it confirm about the man? And what does it tell us about Jesus?

10. How do the herdsmen respond to what Jesus does, and what is the result?

11. What is the response of the people who see the infamous man now in his right mind and hear how it happened?

12. Why do you think they ask Jesus to leave?

13. How does the man who had been tormented by the demons respond to Jesus?

14. What does Jesus tell the man to do?

15. What does the man do, and what is the result?

16. How would you explain the striking contrast between the reaction of the demoniac and the reaction of the Gerasenes?

17. Jesus forbade the leper in Mark 1:44 to tell anyone of his healing, but here he tells the demoniac to tell everyone. What differences in the regions and crowds surrounding the leper and the demoniac could explain Jesus' actions?

18. Go back and read the description of the demoniac. In what ways have you been like him in bondage to your sin? From what has Jesus delivered you?

19. What is your reaction to this deliverance? Are you telling "everyone"?

Day 3

Pray, then read Mark 5:21–43.

Mark 5:21–43

1. What happens to Jesus when he crosses to the other side of the sea?

2. Who comes to Jesus? What is special about this man, and how does he behave toward Jesus?

3. What does the man ask of Jesus?

4. How does Jesus respond?

5. Describe the scene as Jesus goes with Jairus:

6. How is the woman in the next verses described?

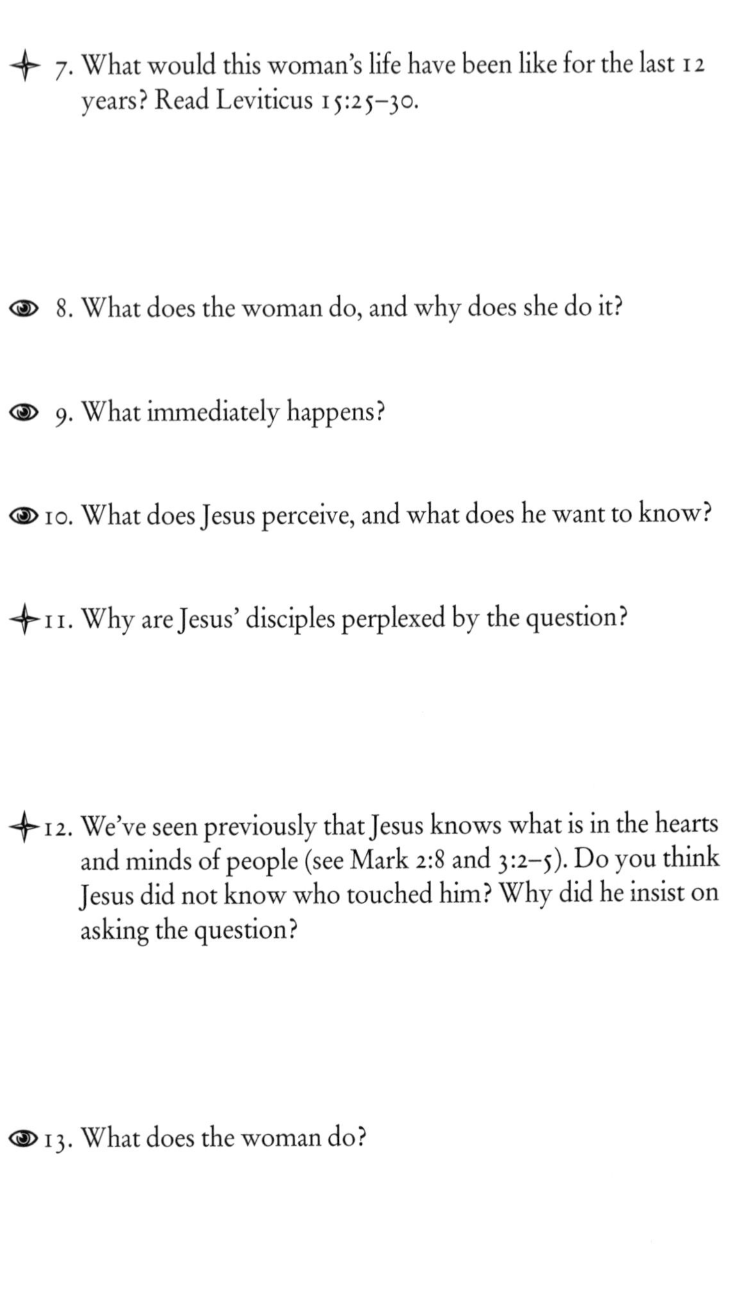

7. What would this woman's life have been like for the last 12 years? Read Leviticus 15:25–30.

8. What does the woman do, and why does she do it?

9. What immediately happens?

10. What does Jesus perceive, and what does he want to know?

11. Why are Jesus' disciples perplexed by the question?

12. We've seen previously that Jesus knows what is in the hearts and minds of people (see Mark 2:8 and 3:2–5). Do you think Jesus did not know who touched him? Why did he insist on asking the question?

13. What does the woman do?

14. Why does the woman approach Jesus in fear and trembling?

15. What does Jesus say to the fearful woman when she confesses?

16. How do you think the woman felt after Jesus spoke these words to her? What specifically in his words would make her feel this way?

17. Looking back over verses 24–33, what words and actions indicate the woman's faith in Jesus?

18. How is this woman's healing a picture of salvation?

19. If you are a Christian, what similarities do you see between what Jesus has done for this woman and what he has done for you?

20. How does this passage give you hope for hopeless women and motivate you to share Jesus with them?

Day 4

Pray, then read Mark 5:21–43.

Mark 5:21–24 and 35–43

1. As you reread Mark 5:21–24, what stands out to you about Jairus?

2. How do you think Jairus feels as the crowds "throng" around Jesus, and Jesus takes the time to interact with a woman?

3. What news does Jairus hear in verse 35?

4. How does Jesus react to the news?

5. What is Jesus asking Jairus to believe?

6. Why would believing be the antidote for fear?

7. Who does Jesus allow to come with him?

8. What does Jesus see when he gets to Jairus' house?

9. Some of the mourners would have been professionals brought in for the funeral. What does Jesus tell them about the girl, and what is their reaction?

10. What does their reaction tell us?

11. Why do you think Jesus puts everyone but the child's parents and Peter, James, and John outside?

12. What does Jesus do in verse 41?

13. How does the dead girl react?

✦ 14. What does this account show that Jesus has authority over?

👁 15. What are Jesus' instructions in verse 43?

✦ 16. Why do you think Jesus charges them not to tell anyone about this stupendous miracle?

✦ 17. In first century Palestine, women and children were not highly valued. What does it tell you about Jesus that he would go out of his way to heal this little girl?

✦ 18. Touching a dead person caused ceremonial uncleanness for Jews. Likewise, the touch of a woman with a discharge of blood would make one unclean. Why was Jesus not made ceremonially unclean by these encounters?

♥ 19. Some people feel they need to clean up their lives for Jesus to accept them? How would you use the accounts of the woman with the discharge of blood and Jairus' daughter to address this road-block to trusting in Jesus?

♥ 20. Jesus has the power to raise the dead! How does this account give us hope as we struggle with bodily ailments and age?

♥ 21. How does Jesus' power over death give you comfort when a loved one dies in the Lord?

Day 5

Pray, then read Mark 4:35–5:43.

✦ 1. Summarize each of the accounts of this week in one sentence and sum up in another sentence what you learn about Jesus from the account.

✦ Mark 4:35–41:

✦ **Mark 5:1–20:**

✦ **Mark 5:21–24 and 35–43:**

✦ **Mark 5:24–34:**

♥ 2. We've seen Jesus has authority over people, demons, sin, sickness, and nature. We even see he has authority over death itself. If someone asked you, "Who is Jesus?", how would you answer?

♥ 3. Have you relinquished the illusion of having authority over your own life and put your trust in Jesus? Explain.

♥ 4. What are the areas of your life that you still want to control? Confess these to the Lord.

Notes

Notes

Week 8

Day 1 **Mark 6:1-52**

Pray this week to be captivated by Jesus and rely more deeply on God's word.

Pray, then read Mark 5:41–6:13.

Mark 6:1–6

1. Where does Jesus go with his disciples, and what does he do?

2. Describe how the people from Jesus' hometown react to his teaching:

3. Roman Catholics believe that Mary remained a virgin after Jesus was born. What in this text and Mark 3:31 gives evidence to the contrary?

4. Why do the people take offense at Jesus?

5. What does Jesus say to them?

6. What does the text say Jesus could not do there, and what does it say that Jesus does do?

7. At what does Jesus marvel?

8. Why do you think Jesus marveled at their unbelief?

9. The text suggests that Jesus was unable to do a mighty work in his hometown because of the people's unbelief. Tell whether you think each of the following is true or false, and why?

   a. Faith is the power by which people are healed so people must have faith in order for Jesus to have the power to perform mighty works.

   b. It is not God's will for Jesus to do mighty works where there is unbelief and offense taken at Jesus.

   c. Jesus' mighty works are signs pointing to who he is. He doesn't do miracles on demand or to entertain people.

10. Many historical biographies record only the triumphs of the main character. Why would Mark include this rejection of Jesus?

11. While Jesus did not do mighty works, what does he continue to do?

12. Why would Jesus continue to teach to people without doing mighty works?

13. Jesus' priority is teaching, telling people about the kingdom of God. How can you prioritize this in your life?

14. If a friend told you she needed to see a miracle to believe in God, how would you respond?

13. Some faith-healing movements tell people that if they believe strongly enough that they will be healed, they will be healed. What is the problem with this teaching?

Day 2

Pray, then read Mark 6:1–20.

Mark 6:7–13

1. What does Jesus do with the twelve?

2. How does he send them out?

3. Why do you think that Jesus sent the disciples out without any supplies?

4. Jesus' disciples had to trust him and rely on others' hospitality as they went out. Describe a particular time in your life when you have had to trust Jesus to provide for you?

♥ 5. The reality is that God provides "life and breath and everything" (Acts 17:25) for us every day. In what ways can we acknowledge this in our daily lives?

👁 6. What does Jesus instruct the disciples to do in each village?

✦ 7. Jesus tells the disciples how to deal with rejection. How do you think the rejection of Jesus in his own hometown prepared the disciples for what they would go through?

👁 8. What do the disciples proclaim, and what signs accompanied this proclamation?

✦ 9. We've seen John the Baptist call people to repentance (Mark 1:4). We've seen Jesus urge people to repent (Mark 1:15). Now Jesus' twelve disciples are proclaiming repentance. What does it mean to repent, and why is it fundamental to the gospel?

♥ 10. What does repentance look like in your life?

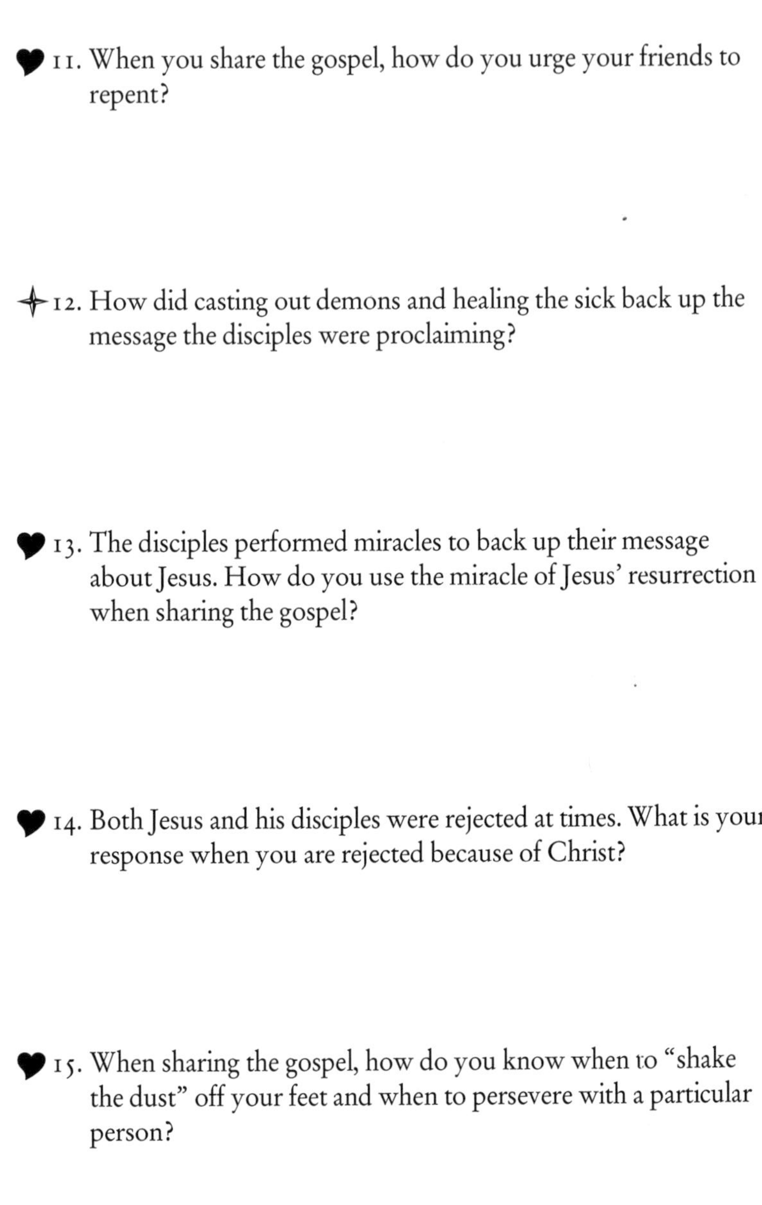

♥ 11. When you share the gospel, how do you urge your friends to repent?

✦ 12. How did casting out demons and healing the sick back up the message the disciples were proclaiming?

♥ 13. The disciples performed miracles to back up their message about Jesus. How do you use the miracle of Jesus' resurrection when sharing the gospel?

♥ 14. Both Jesus and his disciples were rejected at times. What is your response when you are rejected because of Christ?

♥ 15. When sharing the gospel, how do you know when to "shake the dust" off your feet and when to persevere with a particular person?

Day 3

Pray, then read Mark 6:7–29.

Mark 6:14–29

1. King Herod was the Roman appointed ruler of Galilee. What did he hear about?

2. What was being said about Jesus, and what did Herod believe?

3. Why had Herod put John the Baptist in prison?

4. Why did Herod keep John safe for a time?

5. How did John's beheading come about?

6. How did Herod feel about John's beheading, and why didn't he stop it?

7. Verse 20 tells us that Herod was perplexed by John's teaching but still gladly listened to him. What was more important in Herod's life than John's teaching?

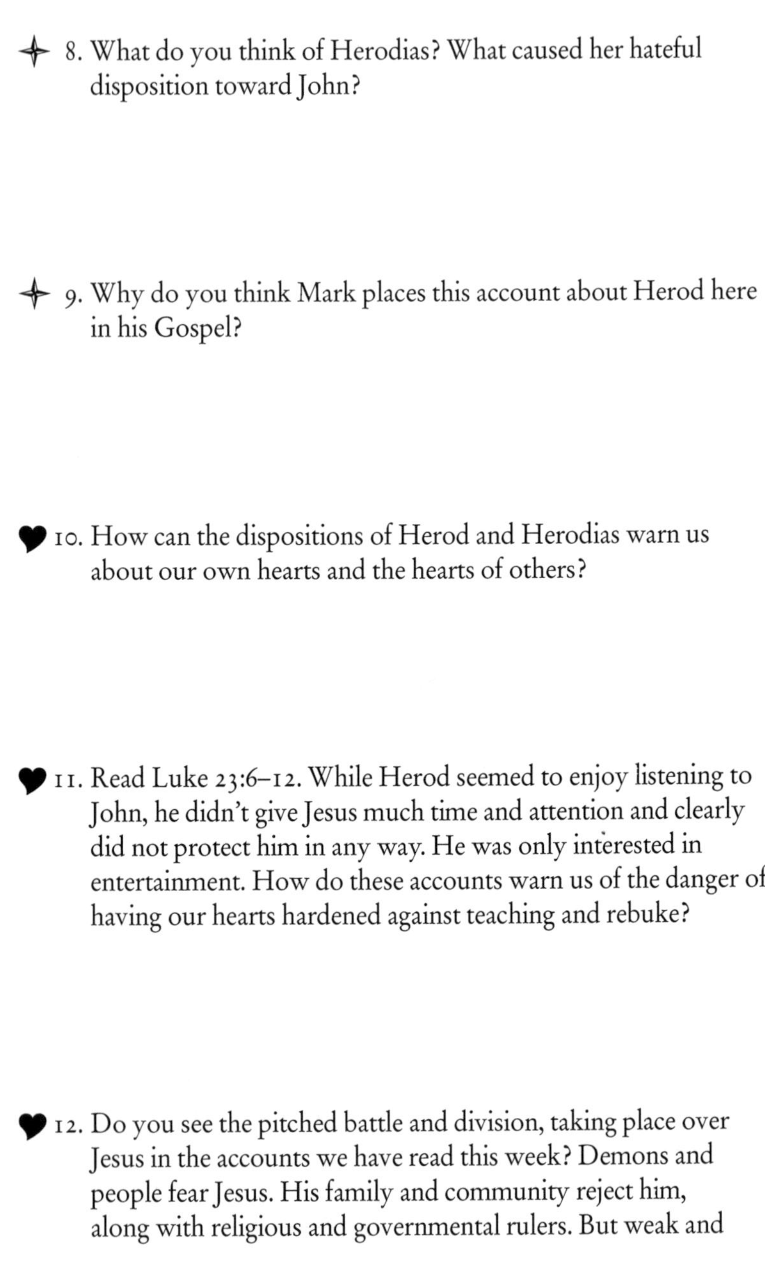

✦ 8. What do you think of Herodias? What caused her hateful disposition toward John?

✦ 9. Why do you think Mark places this account about Herod here in his Gospel?

♥ 10. How can the dispositions of Herod and Herodias warn us about our own hearts and the hearts of others?

♥ 11. Read Luke 23:6–12. While Herod seemed to enjoy listening to John, he didn't give Jesus much time and attention and clearly did not protect him in any way. He was only interested in entertainment. How do these accounts warn us of the danger of having our hearts hardened against teaching and rebuke?

♥ 12. Do you see the pitched battle and division, taking place over Jesus in the accounts we have read this week? Demons and people fear Jesus. His family and community reject him, along with religious and governmental rulers. But weak and needy people put their trust in him. How have you seen or experienced this kind of division over Jesus?

Day 4

Pray, then read Mark 6:7–13 and 30–44.

Mark 6:30–44

1. The apostles return to Jesus. What had they been doing and teaching?

2. When the apostles return, what does Jesus tell them to do, and why?

3. What do Jesus and his apostles do, and how are their plans thwarted?

4. How does Jesus react to the crowds, and why?

5. What does Jesus begin to do?

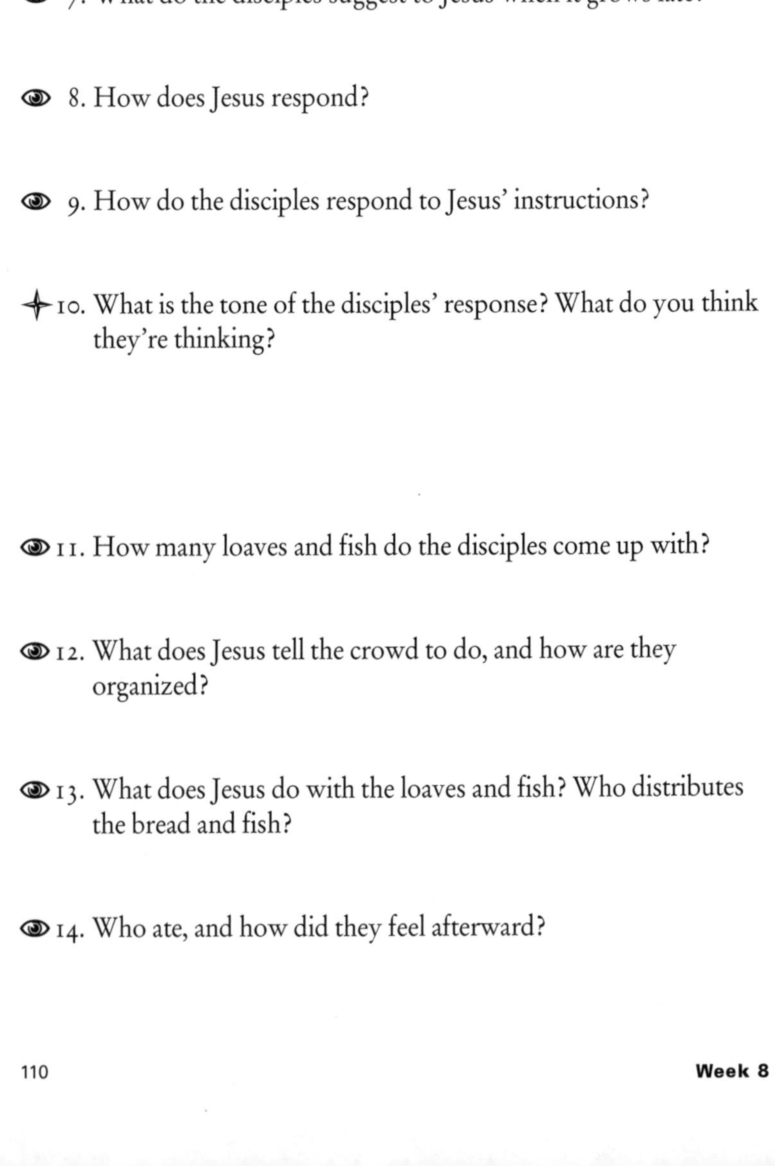

6. What does this tell you about Jesus and his priorities?

7. What do the disciples suggest to Jesus when it grows late?

8. How does Jesus respond?

9. How do the disciples respond to Jesus' instructions?

10. What is the tone of the disciples' response? What do you think they're thinking?

11. How many loaves and fish do the disciples come up with?

12. What does Jesus tell the crowd to do, and how are they organized?

13. What does Jesus do with the loaves and fish? Who distributes the bread and fish?

14. Who ate, and how did they feel afterward?

15. How much was leftover, and how many men had eaten the loaves?

16. What had Jesus done with the five loaves of bread and the two fish?

17. What would the people have remembered from their history when Jesus, after teaching them, did this stupendous miracle? Read Deuteronomy 8:3, 10.

18. How could Jesus multiply such a small amount of food into enough to feed five thousand men?

19. What does this account tell us about Jesus as the shepherd of his sheep? (See also Ezekiel 34:1–16.)

20. What is the significance of Jesus telling his disciples to give the crowd something to eat and then giving the bread and fish to his disciples to set before the people? Is it just a practical

way of distribution or is this account an acted out parable of something? See John 15:26–27, 21:17 and Ephesians 2:19–20.

✦ 21. How is this real life parable evidence for the authority of Scripture?

♥ 22. If you are one of Jesus' sheep, what does this parable tell you about the importance of Scripture in your life?

♥ 23. In what ways do you make sure you are fed and satisfied by God's word?

♥ 24. How does this passage increase your confidence in Jesus' ability to care for you spiritually and physically?

Day 5

Pray, then read Mark 6:30–56.

Mark 6:45–52

1. Why did Jesus have his disciples go across to Bethsaida without him?

2. What does Jesus' seeking times of private prayer tell you about him?

3. How do you prioritize private times of prayer?

4. What does Jesus see happening to the disciples on the boat?

5. What, then, does Jesus do?

6. What is the disciples' reaction when they see Jesus walking on the water, and why do they react this way?

7. What does Jesus say to the disciples?

8. What happens when Jesus gets into the boat?

9. How do the disciples react to the situation, and why?

10. What does Jesus' ability to walk on water show about him? See also Job 9:8.

11. What might the disciples be reminded of by Jesus' words in verse 50? See Deuteronomy 31:6; and Isaiah 41:13–14, and 43:1–3.

12. What prior event would the disciples remember when the wind suddenly ceased?

13. How does the disciples' fear and amazement betray their lack of understanding? What don't they understand?

✦ 14. What do hardened hearts have to do with lack of understanding? Why does Mark say the disciples' hearts were hardened?

♥ 15. Are there ways that your heart is hardened? Are there any biblical or theological issues about which you lack understanding because you don't want to learn?

♥ 16. How can you work to have a soft, teachable heart?

✦ 17. There are several interesting facts in this passage. First, Jesus "made" his disciples get into a boat knowing that it would be impeded by wind. Second, it seems that Jesus saw the disciples struggling in the evening, but he didn't get to them until between 3:00 and 6:00 A.M. the next morning. Third, Jesus "meant to pass by them," but helped after they were terrified and cried out. How would you explain Jesus' reason for doing these things? Was he trying to teach the disciples something?

♥ 18. Just as Jesus told his disciples “Take heart; it is I” in verse 50, he tells them in Matthew 28:10, “Behold, I am with you always, to the end of the age.” If you are Jesus’ disciple, how do these assurances of Jesus’ presence help you when you are “making headway painfully”?

♥ 19. How can you keep an awareness of the presence of Jesus so that you trust his nearness at difficult times?

Notes

Week 9

Day 1 **Mark 6:53-7:30**

This week, pray for the ability to see the depths of your sin and give praise for Jesus' ability to heal you.

Pray, then read Mark 6:45–7:13.

Mark 6:53–56

1. What happens when Jesus and his disciples reach the shore that morning?

2. Where are the people gathering to see Jesus?

3. How are many people healed?

4. What is Mark showing in these few verses?

5. What do these verses tell you about those who come to Jesus?

6. Which do you feel: needy or self-sufficient? Why do you need Jesus?

Day 2

Pray, then read Mark 7:1–23.

Mark 7:1–13

1. Who now gathers around Jesus, and what do they notice?

2. In contrast to Jesus' disciples, what is the tradition of the elders?

3. What do the Pharisees and scribes ask Jesus?

4. Does Jesus answer their question?

5. How many times is "tradition" mentioned in verses 1–13? And what does Jesus contrast tradition with? What point is Mark making by repeating these words and phrases?

6. The Pharisees and scribes question Jesus about his disciples not following tradition. What does Jesus use to confront them?

7. Jesus quotes Isaiah 29:13. Look at the quote and read Isaiah 29:13. Why is their worship in vain?

8. What does Jesus call these religious leaders in Mark7:6, and what does he accuse them of in verse 8?

9. What example of "rejecting the commandment of God in order to establish your tradition" (v. 9) does Jesus use? Summarize it in your own words.

10. Whom does this tradition benefit and whom does it harm?

11. Have you heard religious teaching that clearly benefitted the religious teacher and harmed the hearers (for example, prosperity gospel televangelists)? What has your experience with this type of teaching been?

12. In verse 13, what does Jesus accuse the religious leaders of doing to the word of God with their tradition?

13. How does Jesus feel about this hypocrisy? What is the tone of this passage?

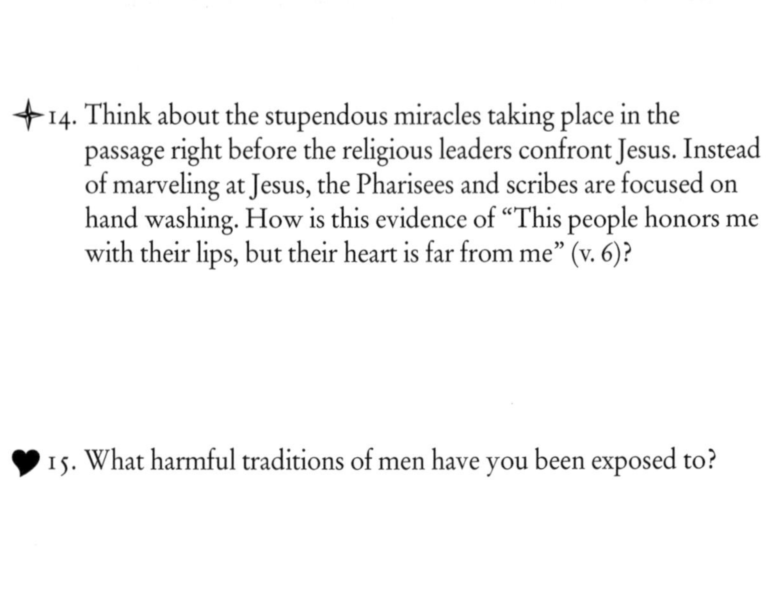

14. Think about the stupendous miracles taking place in the passage right before the religious leaders confront Jesus. Instead of marveling at Jesus, the Pharisees and scribes are focused on hand washing. How is this evidence of "This people honors me with their lips, but their heart is far from me" (v. 6)?

15. What harmful traditions of men have you been exposed to?

16. Are there any traditions in your church, home, or heart that you may be elevating above the word of God?

17. How can you guard against being taken in by traditions of men?

Day 3

Pray, then read Mark 7:1–23.

Mark 7:14–23

1. Whom does Jesus call to himself, and what does he tell them?

2. When Jesus is alone with his disciples, what do they ask him?

3. What is the first thing Jesus says back to the disciples?

4. Why would the disciples have a hard time understanding that defilement or uncleanness doesn't come from what you touch or eat? (See also Leviticus 11:1–47.)

5. Summarize how Jesus explains the parable to his disciples:

6. In his explanation, what does Jesus declare clean? Why is this statement in parenthesis?

7. What does it mean for evil to come out of the heart? And what does this say about the human heart?

8. How do the things Jesus lists defile a person, and what is the result of that defilement?

9. If our very hearts are defiled, what is the remedy? How can we be washed clean if the evil is on the inside? Are there any passages we've already read in Mark that help us with this answer?

10. How could you use these verses to explain how sin separates us from God to someone who believes that the mistakes she has made will likely be forgiven if she does enough good?

11. Some teach a "Devil made me do it" theology that basically says sin comes from bondage to a demon. (For example, if you struggle with coveting the possessions, talents, or lifestyle of others, it is because a demon of covetousness has you in chains. The remedy, therefore, is rebuking the demon as opposed to thankfulness for what you have been given and remembering that Jesus is your greatest treasure.) How would you address "Devil made me do it" theology using what Jesus has said in this passage?

Day 4

Pray, then read Mark 7:14–30.

Mark 7:24–30

1. Where does Jesus go next?

2. Tyre and Sidon are Gentile (non-Jewish) regions. For what reason does Jesus go there? Is there anything in the text that suggests why?

3. Who comes to Jesus, and what does she do?

4. What does Jesus say to this Gentile woman?

5. Whom do the "children" represent, and whom do the "dogs" represent?

6. What does Jesus mean by this statement?

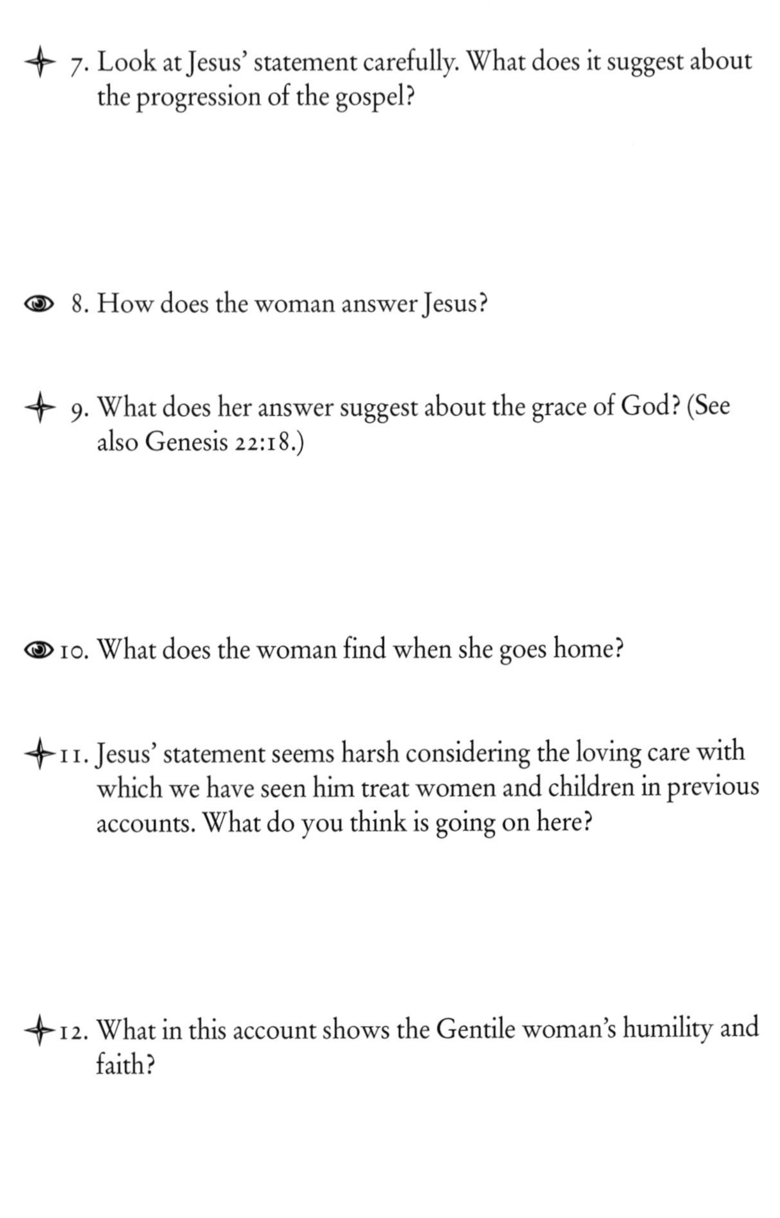

7. Look at Jesus' statement carefully. What does it suggest about the progression of the gospel?

8. How does the woman answer Jesus?

9. What does her answer suggest about the grace of God? (See also Genesis 22:18.)

10. What does the woman find when she goes home?

11. Jesus' statement seems harsh considering the loving care with which we have seen him treat women and children in previous accounts. What do you think is going on here?

12. What in this account shows the Gentile woman's humility and faith?

♥ 13. Examine your own heart. When you go to Jesus with your needs and desires, do you go with an attitude of entitlement or with humility and faith like the Syrophoenician woman?

✦ 14. How did the cross change relations between Jews and Gentiles? See Ephesians 2:11–21.

♥ 15. In eternity, people from every tribe, tongue, and nation will worship around the throne of God because of what Jesus has done. Do you have relationships with people from other cultures that will last into eternity? How can you work to cultivate these types of relationships?

♥ 16. Are you sharing the gospel with people from other cultures? What can you do to open yourself up to more of these opportunities?

Day 5

Pray, then read Mark 7:1–10.

1. David Helm, a preacher and teacher of preaching, talks about "Staying on the Line" of Scripture. The phrase means that we should neither add to nor subtract from a text of the Bible. How did the Pharisees in verses 7–13 add to Scripture? How did they subtract from Scripture?

2. What is dangerous about a Bible teacher adding to or subtracting from the Bible?

3. When sitting under Bible teaching, how can you make sure the teacher is not adding or subtracting from the text of Scripture?

4. Why do you think Mark puts the accounts in verses 1–13, 14–23 and 24–30 next to each other? How are they connected?

✦ 5. How would you contrast the Pharisees, Jesus' disciples, and the Syrophoenician Woman?

♥ 6. Whom would you say you are more like?

♥ 7. How can you examine your heart after reading these passages?

Notes

Notes

Week 10

Day 1 **Mark 7:31–8:26**

Begin each day by asking God to open your eyes and increase your understanding.

Pray, then read Mark 7:24–8:10.

Mark 7:31–37

1. Where does Jesus go after returning from Tyre and Sidon?

2. Who is brought to Jesus, and what is asked of him?

3. What does Jesus do?

4. What happens after Jesus says, "Ephphatha"?

5. How is this healing different from the other healings we have read about in Mark?

6. We don't know for sure why Jesus put his fingers into the man's ears and touched his tongue with his spittle. It may be that he was using means for healing that the people in the region understood. It may be that he wanted the people to recognize their need for his healing touch. Ultimately, it was at the command of Jesus, "Ephphatha," that the man's ears were opened and his tongue was released. What do you think Jesus

was showing his disciples by healing this deaf and mute man, especially in light of his statements in Mark 7:18 and 8:17–18? (Notice, this account is sandwiched between these discussions with his disciples.)

♥ 7. Do you feel your need for Jesus to enable you to understand spiritual things? How do you show your reliance on him for understanding?

✦ 8. Why do you think Jesus sighs before healing this man? What saddens him about the state of the deaf and mute man?

♥ 9. There is no suggestion in this account that this man's disabilities were directly caused by his or someone else's sin. But the effects of the fall have been far reaching, tainting all of creation. Jesus' sigh shows the compassion he feels for mankind in our weak, sin-tainted state. Do you mourn over sin's effects in the lives of other people? Tell about a time when you "sighed" over the effect of the fall.

10. What does Jesus charge the people, and what do they do?

11. What is the response of the people who hear of the healing?

12. What is the significance of the statement, "He even makes the deaf hear and the mute speak" in light of Isaiah 35:4–6? What are people wondering about Jesus?

13. Considering Isaiah 35:4, what would people expect from Jesus if he is the Messiah? How does this explain Jesus' charge to keep this healing quiet but the people continuing to zealously proclaim it?

14. Are you personally thankful that Jesus is so much more than just a political messiah? If so, why?

Day 2

Pray, then read Mark 8:1–21.

Mark 8:1–9

1. Where is Jesus when a great crowd gathers, and how long does the crowd stay with him?

2. Why does Jesus want to feed the crowd?

3. How do the disciples respond to Jesus' desire to feed the crowd?

4. How many loaves and how many fish do the disciples have?

5. What does Jesus do with the loaves and the fish?

6. How many people ate, and how much was left over?

7. How were the people feeling after eating?

8. The disciples had already experienced the feeding of the 5,000. Why do you think they responded the way they did to Jesus' desire to feed this crowd?

9. The crowd is satisfied and there are seven baskets left over. What does this symbolize?

✦ 10. Jesus performs this stupendous miracle in Gentile territory. What is he signaling?

♥ 11. Jesus is all-satisfying with plenty left over (see Psalm 81:10), yet his disciples still don't ask him to meet their and others' needs. How have you been like the disciples?

♥ 12. When you speak to others about Jesus, how do you convey that he is all-satisfying for everyone, regardless of race, nationality or religious background?

Day 3

Pray, then read Mark 8:1–21.

Mark 8:10–13

👁 1. What does Jesus do after sending away the crowd and who shows up in Dalmanutha?

👁 2. What do the Pharisees begin to do, and what do they seek?

3. Why do they seek a sign from heaven?

4. The Pharisees have seen Jesus heal people and cast out demons. If they weren't eyewitnesses to Jesus' miracle of feeding the 5,000, then they certainly had heard about it. What do the Pharisees want to see in addition to these miracles? What do they mean by "a sign from heaven"? See Luke 21:11, 25–26.

5. How does Jesus respond to the Pharisees?

6. What does it mean that Jesus "sighed deeply in his spirit," and why did he react this way?

7. What Jesus mean when says that "no sign will be given to this generation"? (He has already done so many miracles, and John in his Gospel actually calls the miracles signs.) What is Jesus saying he will not do?

8. What does Jesus do in verse 13?

✦ 9. Why does Jesus refuse to prove himself by giving the Pharisees a sign?

♥ 10. Some today pray fervently for "sign and wonders" to prove to unbelievers there is a God. Why is this unnecessary and even unhelpful? (See also Mark 13:22.)

♥ 11. What are the ordinary means God uses to open people's eyes and cause them to believe?

♥ 12. What about when you or a friend has doubts? What do you pray for and remind yourself or your friend?

Day 4

Pray, then read Mark 8:1–21.

Mark 8:14–21

1. Who has forgotten to bring bread, and how much do they have with them?

2. What does Jesus caution the disciples?

3. What do the disciples discuss with one another?

4. After Jesus first asks the disciples why they are discussing their lack of bread, what series of questions does he then ask them?

5. What two events does Jesus remind his disciples of?

6. What does Jesus emphasize about these two events, and why do you think he emphasizes this?

7. With what question does Jesus conclude?

8. When the subject of bread is brought up, Jesus takes the opportunity to teach his disciples. What do the disciples think Jesus is talking about when he warns them about the "leaven" of the Pharisees and Herod?

✦ 9. Considering Jesus' recent interaction with the Pharisees, the passage about Herod and John the Baptist (Mark 6:14–29) and disciples' current struggles, what does Jesus really mean by the "leaven" of the Pharisees and Herod? (See also Matthew 16:12.)

✦ 10. What does leaven do to bread, and why would Jesus warn his disciples in this way?

♥ 11. How can you heed Jesus' warning and beware of false teaching or legalism?

✦ 12. What does Jesus mean when he suggests that the disciples have eyes but don't see and ears but don't hear? And what does this have to do with having a hardened heart?

✦ 13. Keeping in mind that Jesus asks the disciples to remember his feeding multitudes of people with plenty left over, what are the disciples yet to understand?

♥ 14. Some encourage a "leap of faith" to believe in Jesus which suggests believing without understanding. Others would base their faith mainly on what makes them feel good. What does understanding have to do with faith, and how can you strengthen your faith through understanding?

♥ 15. Did you notice the difference in focus between Jesus and his disciples? Jesus was concerned about the disciples' spiritual health while the disciples were worried about their stomachs. How would you describe the focus in your life, especially when you consider your conversations with others and your prayers?

♥ 16. How can you work to refocus the areas of your life that are not centered on Jesus?

♥ 17. In the feedings of the multitudes, Jesus fed thousands and they went away satisfied, leaving baskets full of leftovers. How can you rely more fully on Jesus to abundantly satisfy you?

Day 5

Pray, then read Mark 7:31–37 and 8:14–26.

Mark 8:22–26

1. Where does Jesus go with his disciples, and who is brought to him?

2. What do the people beg Jesus to do, and where does Jesus take the blind man?

3. What does Jesus do first?

4. What does Jesus ask the man, and how does the man answer?

5. What does Jesus do next, and what is the result?

6. Where does Jesus send the man, and what does he tell him to avoid?

7. How is this healing different than any of the other healings we have read about?

8. What means does Jesus use to heal the blind man in two steps?

9. Considering Jesus' discussion with his disciples in verses 14–21, how is this healing an acted out parable for Jesus' disciples?

10. The disciples seem pretty clueless about what Jesus has come to do. What is their only hope for having their eyes opened to full understanding?

11. What does this tell us about what we need to truly understand Jesus?

12. How can we be touched by Jesus in a way that opens our eyes? (What means does he use today to open our eyes?)

13. This week we have seen Jesus open the ears of a deaf man and open the eyes of a blind man. We have seen Jesus satisfy the hunger of thousands and refuse to prove himself to hypocritical religious leaders. We have heard him urge his disciples to hear, see, and understand. How can you increase your understanding of who Jesus is, what he has done, and what he wants from you?

Notes

Notes

Week 11

Day 1 **Mark 8:27–9:13**

Pray this week to see clearly who Jesus is and to be willing to deny yourself, take up your cross, and follow him.

Pray, then read Mark 8:22–9:1.

Mark 8:27–30

1. Where did Jesus go, and whom did he take with him?

2. What did Jesus ask his disciples?

3. What do they tell Jesus?

4. Who was John the Baptist, and why would people say that Jesus is John the Baptist?

5. Who was Elijah, and what would it mean to the Jews if Jesus was Elijah? Read Malachi 4:5–6. (See also 1 Kings 16:29–19:18 and 2 Kings 1:1–2:14.)

6. Why would some Jews think Jesus was a prophet, and what would that mean for them? Read Deuteronomy 18:15–18.

7. What does Jesus ask his disciples next?

8. Who answers, and how does he answer?

9. What does Peter mean when he calls Jesus the Christ? See 2 Samuel 7:8–16; Psalm 2; and Jeremiah 23:5–6.

10. What does Jesus strictly charge his disciples?

11. Why do you think Jesus tells his disciples not to tell anyone that he is the Christ? See John 6:14–15.

12. Peter and the other disciples had lived with Jesus, heard him teach, watched him do miracles, and observed his life up close. They believed Jesus was the Christ who would conquer their enemies. Who do you believe Jesus is, and why do you believe it?

13. How does your answer to question 12 affect your life?

Day 2

Pray, then read Mark 8:27–9:1.

Mark 8:31–33

1. In the previous verses, what did Peter confess about Jesus?

2. What does Jesus now begin to teach the disciples?

3. How did Jesus say these things?

4. Who is the Son of Man? (See also Mark 2:10–12, 28.)

5. How does Peter respond to Jesus' teaching?

6. Why does Jesus rebuke Peter for his rebuke?

7. What do you think of Peter rebuking the one whom he has just confessed to be the Christ?

8. Notice that Peter takes Jesus aside to rebuke him, but Jesus turns and seems to rebuke Peter in front of the other disciples. Why do you think Jesus rebuked Peter publicly?

9. On a 1 to 10 scale of harshness, 10 being the harshest, how would you rate Jesus' rebuke of Peter?

10. How is Peter setting his mind on the things of man, and why is that so dangerous?

♥ 11. Do you ever rebuke Christ in your actions or heart, wanting him to give you an easier life or better circumstances?

♥ 12. After reading Jesus' response to Peter, what do you think about your desires to control Jesus in this way?

✦ 13. What would it mean for Peter to set his mind on the things of God? How would he do that?

♥ 14. Peter at this point misunderstood the mission of Jesus Christ. Instead of humbly following Jesus, he thought he knew what Jesus should and should not do. How can you endeavor to understand Jesus and his mission, following him instead of leading the way? How can you make sure your mind is set on the things of God?

15. Spend some time meditating on what it means that Jesus is the Christ, particularly thinking through verse 31. Let this meditation lead you to prayer and praise.

Day 3

Pray, then read Mark 8:29–9:1.

Mark 8:34–38

1. Whom did Jesus call to himself along with the disciples?

2. Look carefully at the first sentence Jesus says. What does it mean to deny oneself?

3. Today, many wear the cross as a piece of jewelry or use it to decorate their homes. But when Jesus told people they must take up their crosses to follow him, the cross was an instrument of torture and death. Only the worst of non-Roman criminals would be executed in this way. What does Jesus mean when he tells anyone who comes after him to "take up his cross"?

✦ 4. What does it mean to follow Jesus?

✦ 5. Look closely at the second sentence Jesus speaks. How does his second sentence relate to and further define his first?

✦ 6. Why would someone who desires to save her life end up losing it? What does Jesus mean?

✦ 7. How would someone lose her life for Jesus and the gospel, and what does Jesus mean when he says that it will result in her saving her life?

✦ 8. What are the answers to the questions in verses 36 and 37? How do these rhetorical questions help explain verse 35?

9. Of whom will the Son of Man be ashamed?

10. When will he be ashamed?

11. What does this have to do with forfeiting one's soul?

12. From verses 34–38, summarize what Jesus is saying about the cost and the benefit of following him.

13. Is there a special category of Christians who are called to deny themselves and lay down their lives for Jesus? Show from the text to whom these verses apply.

14. What does it mean for you personally to deny yourself in following Jesus? In what ways have you denied yourself? In what ways do you need to strive to deny yourself?

♥ 15. Remembering that the cross is an instrument of torture and death, what does it mean for you to take up your cross?

♥ 16. How are you losing your life for Jesus and the gospel's sake?

✦ 17. In verse 38, Jesus warns against being ashamed of him and his words. How was this a warning to Peter and the other disciples in light of what we studied yesterday?

♥ 18. What are ways we can be ashamed of Jesus' words today?

♥ 19. Jesus gives a sober warning in these verses. How can you strive to be built up in the faith so that you are never ashamed of Jesus and his words?

Day 4

Pray, then read Mark 8:27–9:13.

Mark 9:1

1. Jesus has just described the cost of discipleship to all those who would follow him. What does he tell them in Mark 9:1?

2. What does seeing the kingdom of God come with power have to do with the previous verses on following Jesus?

3. What do you think the kingdom of God coming in power could refer to? Write some possibilities and tell what you think is most likely, and why? (Consider that all three of the synoptic Gospels place this statement directly before the transfiguration where Jesus gives three of his disciples a glimpse of his glorious divinity.)

Mark 9:2–13

4. Whom does Jesus lead up to a high mountain?

5. What happens to Jesus?

6. Who appears to them, and what are they doing?

7. What does Peter suggest, and what motivates him to suggest this?

8. What astounding thing happens next?

9. How does the scene end in verse 8?

10. What do Peter, James, and John get a glimpse of when Jesus is transfigured? Read Hebrews 1:3, 2 Corinthians 4:6 and 2 Peter 1:16.

11. Of all the Old Testament saints, why would Elijah and Moses come to meet with Jesus? What did they represent, and what is the point of their speaking with Jesus? See Luke 24:27 and 44, John 1:45 and Matthew 5:17.

12. Why would Peter have wanted to build three tents? What did he think, and what did he not understand?

✦ 13. Read Exodus 24:15–16. In Mark 9:7, what does the cloud represent, and whose voice comes out of the cloud?

✦ 14. To whom does God the Father speak, and what is the significance of his words? (See also Deuteronomy 18:15.)

✦ 15. Peter wants to put up three tents so that Elijah, Moses, and Jesus can all dwell with them. In the Old Testament, God dwelt with his people in the tabernacle (tent) in the Holy of Holies where Moses placed the tablets of the law. This was the place of worship. Elijah never died but was taken up to dwell with God. Yet God rejects Peter's tents and tells the disciples to listen to his beloved Son; and, when the cloud goes away, Jesus alone is left with them. What is God the Father signaling to the disciples about the new dwelling place of God where the people of God will worship?

✦ 16. What does the transfiguration account tell us about who Jesus is? Point to specific verses in your explanation.

✦17. What does the transfiguration account tell us about Jesus' relationship to the Old Testament?

♥ 18. How does Jesus fulfilling the law and the prophets change the way you read your Old Testament?

♥ 19. God the Father is telling us in this account to listen to his Son. How do we do that? Where do we find Jesus speaking, and what does it mean to listen to him?

♥ 20. Are you listening to Jesus? Do you read his word daily and obey what he commands? In what ways would you like to improve your listening?

✦21. In this account we see Jesus in glory and power, but Jesus has just told his disciples in 8:31 that he will suffer and be rejected and killed. How can it be that Jesus had this glory and power and was still mistreated at the hands of men?

22. If you are a follower of Jesus, he calls you to suffer, be rejected, and possibly be killed, but you also look forward to glory. See Mark 8:35 and Romans 8:30. As Christian in John Bunyan's Pilgrim's Progress experienced, the way to glory travels through the valley of suffering. In what ways have you suffered, and how has that suffering prepared you for glory?

23. If you are not currently a follower of Jesus but are considering following him, have you counted the cost of following him? In what ways might you suffer if you decide to follow Jesus?

Day 5

Pray, then read Mark 8:27–9:13.

Mark 9:9–13

1. What does Jesus charge the disciples with as they are coming down the mountain?

2. What do the disciples question?

3. Why do you think Jesus would not want these disciples to tell others about what they saw on the mountain until after he rises from the dead?

4. Why did the idea of Jesus rising from the dead perplex these disciples even though he had already told them that he would "after three days rise again" (Mark 8:31)?

5. What do the disciples ask Jesus?

6. Jesus affirms that Elijah does come. What does Elijah come to do?

7. What is written about the Son of Man?

8. What does Jesus tell the disciples about Elijah?

9. When Jesus says that Elijah has come, about whom is he talking?

✦ 10. How did John the Baptist restore all things? How did he fulfill the Malachi 4:5–6 prophecy? See Malachi 3:1 also.

✦ 11. Read Psalm 22:6–8 and Isaiah 53:2–3. These passages are prophecy about the Christ suffering and being treated with contempt. In what ways did the prophecies come true for Jesus? (You may want to read all of Psalm 22 and Isaiah 53 and write down all the parallels you see to the crucifixion of Jesus.)

✦ 12. John the Baptist experienced suffering and contempt like Jesus and was brutally put to death. Why do you think Jesus connects the coming of Elijah (John the Baptist) with his own suffering and contempt?

✦ 13. Although Jesus ends his discussion with these disciples on a sober note, what does the transfiguration foreshadow that should give the disciples great hope as opposed to leaving them perplexed?

♥ 14. This week we have come to the center of the gospel of Mark, both literally and figuratively. We have heard Peter confess that

Jesus is the Christ. We have listened to Jesus teach that he will suffer, be killed, and rise again and that his disciples must give up their lives to follow him. We have seen Jesus transfigured in power and glory. Is there anything you struggle with in what you have read and studied this week? Be sure to talk these things through in your small group or with someone in your church.

♥ 15. In your studying this week, what has given you hope? What has spurred you on? What has given you joy?

♥ 16. End this first half of the Gospel of Mark study, giving God praise for the things you listed above.

Notes

Notes

Don't miss the concluding volume in this study of Mark...

Son of God

A Bible Study for Women on the Gospel of Mark (Volume 2)

An 11-week study covering Mark 9:14–16:8

http://bit.ly/Mark-Vol2

The best prices, plus automatic bulk discounts, are available at
CruciformPress.com

DELIGHTING IN THE WORD

The Gospel of God: A Bible Study on Romans for Women (Vol. 1 available Summer, 2024) bears the all-new *Delighting in the Word* cover design that will soon be rolled out to all titles in the series!

10 weeks

Joy! (Philippians)

10 weeks

Faith (James)

10 weeks

Grace (Ephesians)

11 weeks

11 weeks

Son of God (Gospel of Mark, 2 volumes)

9 weeks

Zeal (Titus)

Devoted

Great Men and Their Godly Moms

Tim Challies | 128 pages

Women shaped the men who changed the world.

bit.ly/devotedbook

Majoring in Motherhood

A Crash Course in Gospel Truth for the Hardest, Messiest, Most Glorious Job in the World

Emily Schuch | 132 pages

Moms of little ones...here is the joy, humor, and rock-solid encouraging truth you need.

bit.ly/Majoring

Preparing for Marriage

Help for Christian Couples

John Piper | 86 pages

As you prepare for marriage, dare to dream with God.

bit.ly/prep-for-marriage